# Reviews

"Have you ever read a devotion then forgotten about it ten minutes later? I have. But these........these you will not forget. As Iris Yeager brings to you the heart of Jesus, your mind and your heart will wrap around the message and stay within you."

Lisa Lockwood, Christian Service International
Student Support Coordinator

"Iris shares personal insight into God's Word that helps with the everyday application in our lives".

Margaret Hensley, Christian Service
International Finance Director

"Iris' devotions are inspired by our Heavenly Father in ways that each one gives references to situations of daily life. He guides her in the use of scriptures to show His Word can be applied to those situations. She generally leaves you with a challenge to ponder and pray over. Whatever time personal devotions are done, "Yahweh Coffee and Me" is an infusion of encouragement and inspiration."

Cathy Evens, Retired Librarian

"Iris Yeager engages the reader by weaving a thread of life experiences in every devotion that relates to us all and then shows how God, in His everlasting love, guides us on our journey and through those experiences."

Patty Poulson, Retired Educator and Administrator

*To Sandy*

# Yahweh
# Coffee and Me

*Blessings*

*Iris*

### Iris Yeager

WESTBOW
P R E S S®
A DIVISION OF THOMAS NELSON
& ZONDERVAN

WestBow Press books may be ordered through booksellers or by contacting:

WestBow Press
A Division of Thomas Nelson & Zondervan
1663 Liberty Drive
Bloomington, IN 47403
www.westbowpress.com
844-714-3454

Cover by Chris Rush
email address: rushchris@att.net

Margaret Hensley for the photo with "Friends". All others taken by Iris Yeager

ISBN: 978-1-6642-6832-6 (sc)
ISBN: 978-1-6642-6833-3 (hc)
ISBN: 978-1-6642-6831-9 (e)

Library of Congress Control Number: 2022910689

Print information available on the last page.

WestBow Press rev. date: 08/23/2022

# Dedication

I would like to dedicate this book to my late "Aunt Teddy" who saw something special in my writing as a young adult, and to God for making it a reality in this book.

# Acknowledgements

Writing is a very personal and private adventure, however, there are so many people that have had a part in this adventure with me and it would not have been possible without them.

A very special thank you to my son, Chris Rush, for designing such a beautiful cover for "Yahweh Coffee and Me".

Special thanks to Valisha and Katie Cragun, Cathy Evens, Margaret Hensley, Lisa Lockwood, and Rachel Campbell, along with family and friends for their love, support, suggestions, and encouragement through the writing of "Yahweh Coffee and Me".  I cannot thank you enough for taking this journey with me.

# 1

# The Living Word

Delight thyself also in the Lord; and He shall give thee the desires of thine heart.

—Psalm 37:4 (KJV)

As I look back, I am in awe of God and praise Him for the love He has shown me. In reflecting on memories of years gone by, I was so blessed with the privilege of traveling to the Holy Land. Israel was amazing! To be there and walk where Jesus walked was a spiritual high like nothing I have ever experienced. Now, as I read my Bible, it is totally different because it comes alive before my very eyes! It truly is "the living Word."

Acts 7:38 (NIV) says, "He was in the assembly in the wilderness, with the angel who spoke to him on Mount Sinai, and with our ancestors; and he received living words to pass on to us." This is referring to Moses and the way he had received "the tabernacle of the covenant law," which is the Ten Commandments. The people rebelled against what had been given to them, as many of us do today.

We have the most wonderful book ever written, the Bible, but do we truly believe it, or do we pick and choose what we *want* to believe? Second Timothy 3:16 (NIV) says, "All scripture is God-breathed and is useful for teaching, rebuking, correcting and training in righteousness, so that the servant of God may be thoroughly equipped for every good work."

Are you willing to be trained?

Lord, my prayer is that "I have hidden your word in my heart that I might not sin against you" (Psalm 119:11 NIV). I want to be a blessing daily and to love with Your love. Please help me. Amen.

# 2

## Friendship

A friend loves at all times.

—Proverbs 17:17 (NIV)

We all want friends. Proverbs 18:24 (KJV) says, "A man that hath friends must show himself friendly." In other words, if we want friends, we must first be a friend. That says to me we must take the initiative, then God will bless our efforts.

True friends seek a special kind of good for each other—the highest good, which is that they might know God; love Him with all their hearts, souls, and minds; and seek to become the people that God wants them to be.

First Samuel 23:14–18 (KJV) talks about David's relationship with Jonathan, King Saul's son. Jonathan and David were friends. Jonathan was heir to the throne, but David had been anointed to occupy it. Jonathan believed so strongly in God's selection of David, his friend, as king that he helped and encouraged David at great personal cost. David was hiding in the desert of Ziph when he learned King Saul was seeking him to kill him. The significance of this scene is with Jonathan's intent: he was helping David find strength in God.

This is the heart of Christian friendship. Beyond all the things that draw us together as friends is our ambition of sowing God's words of wisdom, refreshing our friends' spirits, and strengthening their grip on God. A true friend is definitely a gift from God and one who continually points us to Him.

Lord, help me be a good friend. Amen.

*Friends (Shari and Iris) looking at the Sea of Galilee*

# 3

# It All Works Together

And we know that all things work together for good to those who love God, to those who are the called according to His purpose.

—Romans 8:28 (NKJV)

We are *all* faced with times of trouble in our lives, but it is up to us how we deal with them. We can use these situations as stepping-stones and trust God for guidance and healing, *or* we can use them as stumbling blocks full of denial and not ask God for help. God can turn it all around for His glory, but only if we love Him and give the situation to Him. God will use all situations to help us, but how does He do that? Through *us*—those of us who want to be His hands and feet. There is always someone out there worse off than we are. When we reach out to someone who is hurting, lonely, or sad, it helps us heal as we take our focus off ourselves and put it back on Christ, where it needs to be.

God will bring deliverance, but only when we give our hurt or problem to Him and then let go and focus on who He wants us to be. Let go and let God!

Thank You, Lord, that You are holding us in the loving embrace of Your eternal strength and presence. Amen.

# I Will Never Leave You

> For He Himself has said, "I will never leave you nor forsake you."
>
> —Hebrews 13:5 NKJV

Please read Hebrews 13:5–6 (NKJV).

Being a widow is a daily struggle for me. I did *not* choose to be alone, so there are times when I feel very lonely. I think, *Where are all my friends? Don't they care? Don't they realize I sometimes need help because I can't do everything by myself?* Living life alone when that is not your choice is difficult, but life is what you make it.

Life is all about choices, and my choice is to live my life the way God wants me to and to glorify Him. I remember what He told me in Hebrews 13:5 (NKJV). Philippians 4:13 (NKJV) says, "I can do all things through Christ who strengthens me."

My cup is half full; I choose to fill it up with Jesus! In so doing, I can love with His love and be a blessing regardless of where I am in life. My daily prayer is to be a blessing to someone and to glorify God in everything I say and do.

Do I fail? Of course I do; I am human. Do I give up or feel sorry for myself? Sometimes, but not for long. When we stay in the Word daily, that is our *living water* that helps restore our souls, and it is our *daily bread* that gives us strength to continue our journey—for Christ.

Dearest Father, thank You for continually reminding us of Your love and Your presence in our lives, especially in the most difficult times. Amen.

# 5

## Don't Kill the Messenger

For the Word of God is living and powerful, and sharper than any two-edged sword, piercing even to the division of soul and spirit and of joints and marrow, and is a discerner of the thoughts and intents of the heart.

—Hebrews 4:12 (NKJV)

When we are saved, our lives change, and we are to live to glorify God: "Therefore, if anyone is in Christ, he is a new creation; old things have passed away; behold, all things have become new" (2 Corinthians 5:17 NKJV). That means we will probably lose some friends but gain others who are also believers because of our common bond—Jesus Christ.

I remember as a child going through growth spurts, which were sometimes physically painful. The adults would say, "They are just growing pains." Well, the same thing happens as we grow spiritually. Sometimes a sermon, Bible study, something a friend says, or something we read in scripture will upset us and may even make us angry.

Hebrews 4:12 (NKJV) says, "For the word of God is living and powerful and sharper than any two-edged sword." Growing can, and probably will, be painful, but it is necessary if we want to be closer to Christ—so don't kill the messenger! They are only doing what God is prompting them to do, trying to be a blessing and a help. The truth more times than not is difficult to hear because it means we might need to change something.

The Bible talks to us about being "salt and light" to the world, bringing God's Word to others. (Please read Matthew 5:13–16 NKJV.) If each believer could reach one person for Christ, what a very different world this would be. Jesus died for us, so we need to live for Him. He will bless us beyond measure.

Lord, use me today to be a blessing to someone. Amen.

# 6

## He Has Plans

This has been my favorite scripture verse since my husband passed away in July 2010. I have been doing short-term mission trips to Jamaica since 2004. When I was there in June of 2010, I felt God telling me I would be there more often. I was excited but at the same time not sure how that was going to happen since I had a husband and a job. So I said to God, "That sounds good to me, but I am not sure how You are going to make that happen—but You are God, and I am just going to trust You."

Unbeknownst to me, in a few short weeks I would become a widow. My loving heavenly Father was giving me something to hold on to when I had to face the most difficult situation of my life—the death of my best friend, my precious husband.

Not only does God have plans for us, but He will never leave us! Hebrews 13:5 (NKJV) says, "For He Himself has said, 'I will never leave you nor forsake you.'" He will walk with us through every situation in life. When we are weak, the Bible says in Isaiah 40:31 (NKJV), "But those who wait on the Lord shall renew their strength;

They shall mount up with wings like eagles, they shall run and not be weary, they shall walk and not faint." When one chapter of our lives ends, a new chapter begins. Will you trust God with the plans He has for you?

Lord, please hold my hand, walk with me daily, and help me be strong. Amen.

# 7

## Words

Please read 2 Timothy 3:14–17 (MSG).

Second Timothy 3:17 (MSG) says, "Through the Word we are put together and shaped up for the tasks God has for us."

Some people do not realize how powerful words are. God's *words* are the way that creation began its existence. In the first chapter of Genesis (NKJV), you will find the phrase "God said" nine times. This is the history of creation. Genesis 1:27 (NKJV) says, "So God created man in His own image, in the image of God He created him; male and female He created them." If we are made in His likeness, or image, our words are powerful as well. Words do one of two things: they give life by edifying, encouraging, and giving hope, or they destroy. We are to do all things to the glory of God, including what we speak. (Please read 1 Corinthians 10:23–24 KJV.)

My grandmother told me, "If you can't say something nice, you shouldn't say anything at all." My grandmother was a Godly woman, and she was sharing wisdom from God's Word with me when I was a young girl.

I also heard later in my adult life that once we have spoken, those words cannot be taken back. If we are hurt and wounded by words, we can heal, but there will always be a scar.

God's Word is life. Jesus says in John 6:63 (NIV), "The Spirit gives life; the flesh counts for nothing. The words I have spoken to you—they are full of the Spirit and life." God's Word is truth. It transforms us and helps us grow spiritually. It is very important we choose our words wisely.

How will you use your words today?

Lord, please help me today to choose words that are pleasing to You and that will encourage the ones who hear them. Amen.

# 8

## What Really Matters.

Are you on the right track? What is God saying to you? Are there things going on in your life that are causing you to look at your priorities? If you have given your life to Christ, these are questions that help us grow spiritually and put us where God wants us—doing His will. As we become closer to Christ, what matters most is not what we want, but what He wants to do through us. First and foremost, He wants us to love Him. Second, He wants us to love people. That is what He is saying in Matthew 22:37–40 (NKJV).

Relationships should always be a priority in our lives. We all make time for the things that are important to us. Too many times we let the busyness of life keep us from the important relationships in life: God, family, and friends. I am retired now, so I have more time to focus on relationships, and I am extremely grateful for that. I spend my mornings with God, and that equips me for the day. In the Bible, it talks about Jesus rising before daylight and going to a solitary place to pray. (Please read Mark 1:35 NKJV.) I find when I put God first in my day, even for a few minutes, my day goes much better.

I am making new friendships, trying to strengthen and enjoy the ones I have had for a while, and spending more time with family. Love is eternal because God *is love!*
First John 4:16 (NKJV) says, "And we have known and believed the love that God has for us. God is love, and he who abides in love abides in God, and God in him." God wants us to love Him and love each other.

What matters most to you?

Lord, help me love with *Your love* today. Amen.

# 9

## Wait

How do you feel when you hear the word *wait*? Anxious, impatient, angry, disturbed, irritable, or any number of other words could describe your feelings at that moment.

We live in a world today that wants everything instantly. Our telephones go with us everywhere, and we can talk to someone halfway around the world at the push of a few buttons. We have microwave ovens that will cook our food in minutes, and the internet can get us any information we want almost immediately. The list goes on.

Are we like that with God? When we need His help and we pray and ask, do we wait patiently for His answer, or do we get tired of waiting and do things our own way, often making matters worse instead of better? Then we become more frustrated and upset and maybe even angry at God for not being there—immediately.

David wrote of how he waited on God, trusting Him in a time of trouble when there seemed to be no explanation or fix coming anytime soon. Instead of giving up, he trusted that he would "see the goodness of the Lord in the land of the living" (Psalm 27:13 NKJV). We need to be encouraged by David and how he waited on God, not giving in to his own will or giving up on God.

I have heard it said, "Patience is a virtue." It is one I know I have to work on regularly, but when we wait on God, it is always the best thing to do. Don't lose heart, but trust God that His timing is perfect; it will be worth the wait.

Will you wait on God like David did, trusting His timing?

Lord, please give me strength to wait for Your answers. Amen.

# 10

## Do Not Be Afraid

For we walk by faith, not by sight.
—2 Corinthians 5:7 (NKJV)

Life is a journey, an adventure God wants us to enjoy, but life is not always easy, happy, and fun. That is why we need to learn to *walk by faith.* Faith is an action word! Faith without obedience is not true faith. When trials come, and they will, we need to put our faith into action and trust God to walk with us through those trials.

When I was much younger in my faith (and in age too) and trials would come, I would become fearful and begin to worry. In Matthew 6:25–34 (NIV), Jesus addresses the issue of worry. In Matthew 6:27 (NIV), Jesus asks, "Can any one of you by worrying add a single hour to your life?" In Matthew 6:34 (NIV), Jesus says, "Therefore do not worry about tomorrow, for tomorrow will worry about itself. Each day has enough trouble of its own." God says in His Word over and over to not be afraid.

If we are worrying and fearful, we are not trusting God. In Mark 4:35–41 (NKJV), Jesus is on the Sea of Galilee with His disciples, and a storm comes; His disciples are afraid. Jesus calms the sea and says in Mark 4:40 (NKJV), "He said to His disciples, 'Why are you so afraid? Do you still have no faith?'" Unfortunately that is one of the faults of us humans. However, as we grow closer to Christ, that can change. Romans 10:17 (NKJV) says, "So then, faith comes by hearing, and hearing by the Word of God." This is another good reason we should read the Bible every day—so we can grow in faith.

A good illustration of *faith* versus *fear* is this:
Picture a light switch with the word *faith* written on the top and *fear* written on the bottom. When *faith* is on, *fear* is off, but when *fear* is on, *faith* is off. The key to a peaceful life is giving God our storms.

How will you walk today? In fear or in faith?

Lord, help me to always trust You and grow closer to You so I can walk by faith. Amen.

*The boat Faith on the Sea of Galilee*

# 11

# Surrender

Life is full of choices. When we go through a difficult time and seek God, we sometimes wear blinders because we want Him to give us the answers we want to hear. Sometimes He gives us answers even when we don't ask a question! Sometimes the answers He gives us seem just too difficult or painful. We try to justify it by saying, "I just feel like I need to pray about it more." Living by how we *feel* can be dangerous because feelings change, but in Hebrews 13:8 (NKJV) the Bible says, "Jesus Christ is the same, yesterday, today and forever."

It has been my experience that God will continue to put the answers in front of us because He loves us so much! He wants us to make the right decisions, the ones that will help us the most, *but*—it is our choice. We can say we have faith that God will help us, but James 2:17 (NIV) says, "In the same way, faith by itself, if not accompanied by action, is dead." We are the ones who have to take that first step and make a decision to surrender our will to God's.

Surrender simply means to yield to another or give up the possession of something to another.

God will never force His choice on us. He gave us a free will to make choices and decisions, but we can never go wrong in choosing what God wants for us, even if it seems too difficult. Surrender to His will because He knows best or continue on your own path—the choice is yours. (Please read John 16:25–33 NKJV.)

If you surrender your life and will to God, that is security for your future, and with that will come peace.

Lord, help me daily to surrender my will to You. Amen.

# 12

## Prayer

This is the confidence that we have in Him, that if we ask anything according to His will, He hears us! And if we know that He hears us, whatever we ask, we know that we have the petitions that we have asked of Him.

—1 John 5:14–15 (NKJV)

Do you believe in the power of prayer? I certainly do. God hears our prayers. We can be sure of that because of what John, the beloved apostle, said in 1 John 5:14–15 (NKJV). He says if we ask *anything*, God hears us. But the scripture also says it has to be "according to His will" (1 John 5:14 NKJV). Therefore, we need to determine what God's will is. We need to be specific and not doubt, ask in faith and pray believing. We need to go to the Father in the name of Jesus (please read Philippians 2:9–11 NKJV) and frame our prayers with the Word of God.

Our prayers are always answered, but not always the way we want. In waiting for God's answer, we are also growing in faith. Psalm 40:1 (NKJV) says, "I waited patiently for the Lord, And He inclined to me, And heard my cry." So He is encouraging us through His Word.

A lot of our prayer life is seeking answers, which we should do, but it should also be about just talking to God, telling Him whatever is on our hearts. He wants a personal relationship with each of us. James 4:8 (NKJV) says, "Draw near to God and He will draw near to you."

It took me a lot of years to understand the scripture in 1 Thessalonians 5:17 (NKJV): "Pray without ceasing." God's Word is profound and living and sometimes difficult to understand. I always thought I could never measure up to what God wanted from me because I could not *pray without ceasing*. What does that even mean? It means being persistent and consistent in prayer. We are to be faithful in our prayer life. God wants a relationship with us, and prayer is an essential part of that. It is how we communicate *with* Him and *to* Him. Communication is the key to every successful relationship, including our relationship to God.

Lord, thank You for the privilege of prayer, that I can talk to You whenever I want to and know that You hear me. Amen.

# 13

## Christchrist Is with Us

Finally, my brethren, be strong in the Lord and in
the power of His might.
—Ephesians 6:10 (NKJV)

Please read Ephesians 6:10–20 (NKJV).

Our Lord will never leave us. He walks beside us, and sometimes He even carries us. He is always with us! He is faithful, and He loves us more than we can comprehend. He is our savior, our brother, and our best friend. We have been adopted into the kingdom of God when we accept Him as our personal savior, so we are joint heirs *with* Christ. This means we are now also fellow laborers with Him. We are His disciples. We are here to be His hands and feet and to spread the gospel.

Romans 10:15 (NKJV) says, "And how shall they preach unless they are sent? As it is written, 'How beautiful are the feet of those who preach the gospel of peace, who bring glad tidings of good things!'" Satan will do all he can do to keep this from happening. He comes against us in many ways: lies, fear, and making us feel as though we don't know enough to do God's work. That is why it is so important that we stay in God's Word and learn.

In Ephesians 6:10–20 (NKJV), it talks about the whole armor of God and what it takes to fight the devil. Ephesians 6:18–20 says (NKJV):

> Praying always with all prayer and supplication in the spirit, being watchful to this end with all perseverance and supplication for all the saints, and for me, that utterance may be given to me, that I may open my mouth boldly to make known the mystery of the gospel, for which I am an ambassador in chains that in it I may speak boldly as I ought to speak.

When we put on the whole armor of God, our whole body is covered except our back, and that is because *God always has our back*! God empowers us through His Word and prayer.

Are you willing to be His ambassador and walk with Him daily?

Lord, please help me to walk with you daily, spreading the gospel to those today who you have chosen to hear it. Amen.

# 14

## God Speaks to Us

And when he brings out his own sheep, he goes before them; and the sheep follow him, for they know his voice.

—John 10:4 (NKJV)

Our God loves us so much! He will speak to us in whatever way it takes to convey His message to us. He speaks to us through His Word and through our circumstances. He may also speak to us through a billboard, something a friend says, or even a verse or saying on a coffee cup. We need to become sensitive to that still small voice inside of us.

I remember once I needed to go to the grocery store, so I started to leave, thinking I had money in my purse. A small voice inside me said, "Get your checkbook." I said to myself, "I am good. I have some cash," so I left without my checkbook. When I got to the checkout at the store and opened my purse ... yep, you guessed it! I remembered I had previously spent the cash for something, and I did not have enough money to pay for my purchases. Totally embarrassed, I asked the clerk to keep what I was buying while I went home for my checkbook. (This was before debit cards!) *I did not listen!* If I had, it would have saved me a trip back home and the embarrassment I experienced.

God starts speaking to us in small ways in the beginning so we can learn to recognize His voice. We need to listen, be sensitive to that voice, and be obedient. In John 10:4 (NKJV), it says, "And when he brings out His own sheep, He goes before them; and the sheep follow him, for they know His voice." We need to learn to hear our Lord's voice and follow Him. Jesus will always lead us in the right direction, through the Holy Spirit.

Will you listen for His voice today?

Lord, please help me to be sensitive and obedient to Your still, small voice speaking to me today. Amen.

# 15

## What Are Your Thoughts.

For as he thinks in his heart, so is he.
—Proverbs 23:7 (NKJV)

How do you think about yourself? What are your thoughts about the person you are? Is your cup half full or is it half empty? Are you a positive person or a negative person? Are you confident or do you have low self-esteem?

The Bible says in Proverbs 23:7 (NKJV), "As a man thinks, so is he." Those are pretty powerful words. There is an old saying, "You are what you eat." Well, according to God's Word, we become the person we *think* we are. We are to grow and become more like Christ, and so we are to think about good and positive things. Satan loves it when he can get us to think about our past sins and how we could not possibly be loved by God because of all the bad things we have done. But Satan is a liar! For every good thing God has for us, Satan has a counterfeit, which he makes look very appealing. In Philippians 4:8–9 (NKJV) it says:

> Finally brethren, whatever things are true, whatever things are noble, whatever things are just, whatever things are pure, whatever things are lovely, whatever things are of good report, if there be any virtue and if there is anything praiseworthy—meditate

on these things. The things which you learned and received and heard and saw in me, these do, and the God of peace will be with you.

When we ask for forgiveness, God forgives *and* forgets our sins. In Hebrews 10:17 (NKJV), the Word says, "Their sins and their lawless deeds I will remember no more." So when we find ourselves thinking wrong, we need to change our thoughts. Praise God for another day, thank Him for something, or say some kind words to someone. We need to honor God with our thoughts as well as our actions.

Lord, please help me to keep my thoughts positive and even prayerful today. Thank You for always helping me when I ask. Amen.

# 16

## Sacrifice

I have been crucified with Christ; it is no longer I who live, but Christ lives in me; and the life which I now live in the flesh I live by faith in the Son of God, who loved me and gave Himself for me.
—Galatians 2:20 (NKJV)

Are you willing to sacrifice your life to live for Jesus? Are you willing to say, "Here I am Lord, send me," or, "Let there be more of You and less of me; let them see You, Lord"? I have heard it said that those who are Christians may be the only *Jesus* some people ever see. We must be willing to do whatever is asked of us and not seek recognition for what we do, only that Jesus be glorified. Sometimes people want to serve, but they want to pick and choose what they do instead of asking God. They then want someone to praise them for the job they have done.

Some people are not willing to do the menial tasks that won't be seen and noticed. They want certain people watching to praise them for the sacrifices they are making to do *God's work*. God has no menial tasks; they are all important, and He is always watching. Look at what Jesus did for *us*! He was born to die for *us* so we could spend eternity with Him. He made the ultimate sacrifice for *us!* Are you willing to live the rest of your life for Him? Are you willing to make a sacrifice for Jesus, so when you meet Him face to face, He will say, "Well done thou good and faithful servant" (Matthew 25:21 NKJV)? That is my goal, to serve my Lord and glorify Him.

What is your goal in life?

Lord, help us to be ever mindful of the sacrifice you made for us. You loved us so much you died for us, so now, please help us to live for you. Amen.

# 17

## Time

But, beloved, do not forget this one thing, that with the Lord one day is as a thousand years, and a thousand years as one day. The Lord is not slack concerning His promise, as some count slackness, but is long-suffering toward us, not willing that any should perish but that all should come to repentance.

—2 Peter 3:8–9 (NKJV)

Time … what are your thoughts about time? Do you want to kill time because you have too much of it? Or do you not have enough so you wish you had more of it? Personally, I do not understand why people want to *kill* time. We need to think about some of the slang terms we use and ask ourselves why we say them. Changing one letter can make the difference between a negative and a positive statement. Instead of to *kill* time, I choose to *fill* it. God has given each of us a certain amount of time to spend here on earth. We do not know when we will be called home to heaven and our time here on earth will be finished.

In 2 Peter 3:8 (NKJV) it says, "But, beloved, do not forget this one thing, that with the Lord one day is as a thousand years and a thousand years as one day." I think through this scripture we are being reminded that our time is *not* the same as God's and how important and precious it is. Things will not always continue as they are. Christ *is* returning someday, and if we do not see that day, our lives here on earth will have ended at some point in time. We need to realize that time is short and there is a lot of work still to do before Christ's return. We need to plan to serve Him as if He is not coming back for a very long time but be ready if He comes today.

What is your choice: to *kill* your time or *fill* your time for the Lord?

Lord, please help me fill the time you have given me to bring glory and honor to You. Amen.

# Sin

> For all have sinned and fall short of the Glory of God.
>
> —Romans 3:23 (NKJV)

We all sin, and that will not change. We are human, but what is most important is that we repent and ask for forgiveness. That is why Jesus came into the world—to set an example and to show us the way to live. In Matthew 18:10–14 (NKJV) is the parable of the lost sheep. If a shepherd has a sheep that goes astray, he leaves the flock and looks for the lost sheep until he finds it, and then he rejoices because he does not want even one to perish. That is the way our heavenly Father looks at us; He wants not one to perish! His desire is for us to accept Christ as our personal savior so we can live with Him in heaven for eternity.

As I am writing this, I am looking out my window, and it is snowing large, beautiful snowflakes, covering the ground with a blanket of snow. In Psalm 51:7 (NKJV), it says, "Wash me, and I will be whiter than snow." It is difficult for me to imagine anything being whiter than snow. When the sun shines on the snow, it is so bright I need to wear sunglasses.

That is what the blood of Jesus will do, wash us and make us whiter than snow. Our sins will be gone, *but* we have to accept that gift.

Salvation is a gift. In order for that gift to be given, there was a price that only Jesus could pay, and He paid that price. Jesus gave the ultimate sacrifice; He gave His life. He died on that cross so we could be forgiven and live with Him in heaven for eternity! That is *love!* He loves each one of us that much. If you were the only person alive, He would have still died for you. That is how much He loves *you!*

Jesus made it easy for us. All we have to do is accept the gift of salvation. If you have never done that, won't you do that today? It is simple: ask Jesus to forgive you of your sins, thank Him for loving you so much and dying for you so you can spend eternity with Him, and then start living for Him because He died for you.

Will you accept Jesus today? Please pray with me: Lord Jesus, please forgive me of my sins. I love You, and I want You to come into my heart. Thank You for loving me so much that You died for me. Now help me to live the rest of my life for You. Amen.

Now go and tell someone you have been saved! The angels in heaven are rejoicing. If you don't go to church, please find one that preaches the Bible and the truth so you can grow to be the person God wants you to be. Read your Bible every day because that is the way God talks to us. Welcome to the family of God!

# 19

## Standing in the gap

So I sought for a man among them who would make a wall, and stand in the gap before Me on behalf of the land, that I should not destroy it; but I found no one.

—Ezekiel 22:30 (NKJV)

Please read Ezekiel 22:23–31 (NKJV).

Think of your home town. Where can I stand in the gap? Who can I show Jesus to? We need to show righteousness and holiness to a lost world. I believe the world looks to Christ's followers for hope. Jesus is the one who stood in the gap for all of us. In Ezekiel 22:30 (NKJV), it says that the leaders were *not* examples of separation from worldly ways as all people of God should be.

The watchman stood on the city wall guarding against any threat, inside or outside of the wall. He would sound an alarm upon sighting impending danger. God made Ezekiel a spiritual watchman over His people. If the watchman failed to give the signal to the city in time of peril, the blood of the city would be required of him. But, if the watchman sounded the alarm and the city did not respond, the watchman could hardly be blamed. As a faithful watchman, Ezekiel would not have placed his own life in jeopardy by failing in his critical duty. A watchman who was asleep on the job would forfeit his life. As Christ followers, we are to be watchmen standing in the gap for others to show them Christ.

Who needs you to "stand in the gap" for them? Are you willing?

Lord, please show me who I need to stand in the gap for today. Amen.

# 20

## Thanksgiving

Enter His gates with thanksgiving and His courts with praise.

—Psalm 100:4 (NIV)

As I sit on the beach looking out at the Caribbean Sea, one of God's beautiful creations, the colors of blue, aqua, and turquoise are vibrant. I am thankful for the time to relax my mind, renew my body, and revive my soul. I am reminded of Psalm 100.

We should thank God for *all* things, both good and bad. When we encounter the bad, we should draw close to Him and thank Him for loving us so much, for never leaving us, and for guiding us through those difficult times. In thanking Him, no matter what the circumstances, we are saying we trust Him. Enjoying the good times is a reward for endurance and obedience. In Philippians 4:6 (NIV) it says, "Do not be anxious about anything, but in every situation, by prayer and petition, with thanksgiving, present your requests to God."

When praying, we need to ask God to show us His will for each new day, then thank Him for it. There is the acceptable will of God and there is the *perfect* will of God. As His children, He wants to give us good things. Psalm 37:4 (NKJV) says, "Delight yourself also in the Lord, and He shall give you the desires of your heart." This verse is saying that when we put God first, He will give us the desires of our hearts. In putting God first, our desires change. I am asking God to show me how to stay in His perfect will for my life.

Where are you with God? Where do you *want* to be with God? Are you living a life of *thanksgiving*?

Father, please help us to always live a life of thanksgiving. Amen.

# 21

## Be Content

Let your conduct be without covetousness; be content with such things as you have. For He Himself has said, "I will never leave or forsake you." So we may boldly say: "The Lord is my helper; I will not fear. What can man do to me?"

—Hebrews 13:5–6 (NKJV)

Today is a bitterly cold winter day with the temperature being two degrees below zero. It is windy, too, so that makes it feel even colder. The winter has been full of many snowy, windy, and bitterly cold days. People have been complaining and saying, "I am so over this nasty weather!" Did you ever want to say to them that perhaps they should move to a warm climate? (In fun, of course!)

The Bible says in Hebrews 13:5 (NKJV), "Let your conduct be without covetousness; be content with such things as you have, for He Himself said, 'I will never leave you nor forsake you.'" Let the warmth of God's love fill you up on those cold winter days.

What kind of lives would we, as believers, really have if we always had everything we wanted, including perfect weather? The challenges we face in everyday life are what make us stronger. God uses every one of them, if we allow Him to, developing us into the people He wants us to become. Even better yet, He *always* walks with us, no matter what. Even on cold days!

Father, sometimes in my weak moments, I complain. Help me to be content today and bring glory and honor to You in everything I do and say. Amen.

# 22

## Lifted Up

And Mordecai told them to answer Esther: "Do not think in your heart that you will escape in the king's palace any more than all the other Jews. For if you remain completely silent at this time, relief and deliverance will arise for the Jews from another place, but you and your father's house will perish. Yet who knows whether you have come to the kingdom for such a time as this."

—Esther 4:13–14 (NKJV)

I was recently in a bible study on the Book of Esther. I knew I was going to learn a lot about Esther's life, but what I did not realize was that I was going to learn a lot about my own life as well. There were times in my life when I refused to let God in because I thought I could do it on my own. It got to the point where I knew I was going to have to make a choice. There were only two choices: turn toward God and give Him my all or completely turn away from Him. There was no more straddling the fence; it was all or nothing!

The first fifty years of my life had a lot of good, but also lots of pain, hurt, and shame. Two failed marriages, a time of rebellion, and other things caused me shame. Sometimes the pain was just too much to bare.

I had wasted so much of my life, but because of God's unconditional love and His forgiveness, I chose, at that critical crossroad in my life, to serve Him—to turn toward Him—to run to Him!

Thank you Lord that you lifted me up (please read Psalm 40:2 NKJV), forgave me, and gave me another chance (please read 1 John 1:9 NKJV). Thank you for having a plan for my life (please read Jeremiah 29:11 NKJV)—"For such a time as this!" (Esther 4:14 NKJV).

If He did it for me, He will do it for you! All you have to do is ask Him.

Father, please forgive me of my sins and draw me close to you. Show me your plan for my life. Amen.

# 23

## Draw Me Close

But He gives more grace. Therefore He says: "God resists the proud, But gives grace to the humble." Therefore submit to God. Resist the devil and he will flee from you. Draw near to God and He will draw near to you. Cleanse your hands, you sinners; and purify your hearts, you double-minded. Lament and mourn and weep! Let your laughter be turned to mourning and your joy to gloom. Humble yourselves in the sight of the Lord, and He will lift you up.

—James 4:6–10 (NKJV)

Growing up, my mom took my brother, sister, and me to church, but my dad never went. When I left home in 1966 after graduating high school, I fell away from God into a worldly life. I went to church off and on, but in 1971 I asked Jesus into my heart and was baptized, still only going to church occasionally. It was in 1984 that I knew something was missing from my life, and I knew it was Jesus. I started attending church again and rededicated my life. In Joshua 24:15 (NKJV), it says, "Choose for yourselves this day whom you will serve."

I realized how foolish it was to try to run my own life and to live the way the world lives. My desires changed, and my heart was transformed. Following God and drawing close to Him gives me purpose and joy. God truly wants to use me, have a relationship with me, and, most of all, love me.

I stopped serving myself and began to serve God. He gave me a passion for missions, so I have been doing short-term mission trips since 2004. I serve in the United States and Jamaica and have served on several extended trips, lasting from four to twelve weeks.

There is no limit to the ways God will use you when you draw close to Him and begin focusing on Him and desiring to serve Him.

Lord, help me today and every day to draw close to You and focus on You. Amen.

# 24

## Run the Race

Do you not know that those who run in a race all run, but one receives the prize? Run in such a way that you may obtain it.

—1 Corinthians 9:24 (NKJV)

My brother and I spend a lot of time every May at the Indianapolis Motor Speedway. Our parents started taking us there in 1962, so we have enjoyed the sport of Indy car racing for a very long time. The excitement of the Indianapolis 500 and all the festivities leading up to it are like none other! It is said to be the greatest spectacle in racing! This is the one race all drivers of this sport aspire to race in and be the winner of and so receive their likeness on the prestigious Borg-Warner Trophy.

As Christ followers, we are also in a race. In Acts 20:24 (NKJV), the Bible says, "But none of these move me; nor do I count my life dear to myself, so that I may finish my race with joy, and the ministry which I received from the Lord Jesus, to testify to the gospel of the grace of God." When we accept Jesus as our personal savior, we are ambassadors for Christ and given the ministry of reconciliation. In 2 Corinthians 5:20 (NKJV), it says, "Now then, we are ambassadors for Christ, as though God were pleading through us: we implore you on Christ's behalf, be reconciled to God." We are running the race for God, testifying of His love and goodness, so that others will repent and be reconciled to Him. Second Timothy 4:7 (NKJV) says, "I have fought the good fight, I have finished the race, I have kept the faith." As Christ followers, at the end of our race, we are all winners. Our prize is heaven and spending eternity with our Lord and Savior, Jesus Christ.

Will you run the race for Jesus Christ?

Lord, we thank You for all you have given us on earth to enjoy while we are here. Help us to run the race for You, so that at the end, our prize will be eternity with You in heaven! Amen.

# 25

## By the Sea

On the same day Jesus went out of the house and sat by the sea.

—Matthew 13:1 (NKJV)

I am sitting on a beach in Florida, which is one of my favorite places in all the world to be for rest and relaxing. I have never met a beach I don't like; I just have my favorite ones. I walk at the edge of the water, which is cool and refreshing on my feet after walking on the warm sand. In the water's edge are many very small fish swimming around. When I return to my beach chair, I watch the sea gulls as they are feeding. They dive very aggressively into the water and come up with small fish. There are several birds doing this, and at one point, one of the birds tries to steal a fish from another bird.

We need to be that intentional about "feeding" on the Word of God. We should be aggressive in seeking spiritual food and then not let Satan try to steal it away from us. In John 6:48 (NKJV), Jesus says, "I am the Bread of Life." In Matthew 4:4 (NKJV), Jesus says, "But He answered and said, 'It is written, 'Man shall not live by bread alone, but by every word that proceeds from the mouth of God.''"

We should apply God's Word to our lives like we apply sunscreen to our bodies at the beach—to protect us.

God can, and will, minister to us and teach us no matter where we are—what better place than in nature, observing all God has so graciously given us to enjoy?

Thank You, Father, for the beauty of nature and for using it to teach us about You. Amen.

*Florida seascape*

# 26

## Trust in the Lord

In You, O Lord, I put my trust; Let me never be put to shame. Deliver me in Your righteousness, and cause me to escape; incline Your ear to me, and save me. Be my strong refuge, to which I may resort continually; You have given the commandment to save me, for you are my rock and my fortress.

—Psalm 71:1–3 (NKJV)

When my youngest son was very young, we lived in Gunnison, Colorado. The mountains were majestic and very beautiful, and they were all around us. I am one who likes adventures, however, sometimes the mountains in our lives are a little more than we can handle. Once I had to drive home from work in Crested Butte during a whiteout snowstorm. I had always wondered what the strange colored poles along the road were, but that day I found out. Those poles were the only things I could see to show me where the road was so I would not drive off the side of the mountain. Psalm 56:3 (NKJV) says, "Whenever I am afraid I will trust in you."

When we look at the mountains behind us, we see how God has brought us safely to the valley. Then, as we look at the mountains ahead of us, we can be assured God will direct us so that we can conquer those as well. *But,* we have to trust Him.

The Word says in Proverbs 3:5–6 (NKJV), "Trust in the Lord with all your heart, and lean not on your own understanding; in all your ways acknowledge Him and He shall direct your paths."

Lord, please help us to trust You today and cast *all* our cares on You. We know You love us and will bring us safely from the mountains of life. Amen.

# 27

## The Everlasting Arms

For I am persuaded that neither death nor life, nor angles nor principalities, nor powers, nor things present nor things to come, nor height nor depth, nor any other created thing, shall be able to separate us from the love of God which is in Christ Jesus our Lord.
—Romans 8:38–39 (NKJV)

Are you going through a difficult time? Do you feel distant from God? The previous verse in Romans should be a great encouragement to you. Once we belong to God, *nothing* can separate us from His love—*nothing*! He is always by our side. If we fall, He is there to catch us. Deuteronomy 33:27 (NKJV) says, "The eternal God is your refuge, and underneath are the everlasting arms; He will thrust out the enemy from before you and will say, 'Destroy!'" Not only will God catch us in His everlasting arms, but He will destroy the enemy coming against us!

In 1 Peter 5:8 (NKJV), the Bible says, "Be sober, be vigilant; because your adversary the devil walks about like a roaring lion, seeking whom he may devour." When we fall, and we will from time to time, God *will* catch us with His everlasting arms, cradle us in His love, and encourage us to go on.

Father, thank You for Your love, Your everlasting arms, and Your Word. Help me to remember that You are always with me. Amen.

# 28

# God Is in Control

"Is God really in control?" The first time my friend said that to me after I made the comment, "God is in control," I was truly shocked. In Genesis 1:26 (NKJV), it says:

> Then God said, "Let Us make man on Our image, according to Our likeness; let them have dominion over the fish of the sea, over the birds of the air, and over the cattle, over all the earth and over every creeping thing that creeps on earth."

God relinquished control when He gave man dominion over all the earth. Dominion means supreme authority or absolute ownership. God values people! We are made in His image to reflect His majesty while we are on earth. God wants us to rule wisely over all He has made. If we do that which is right, we are accepted by God.

In Genesis 4:6–7 (NKJV), it says, "So the Lord said to Cain, 'Why are you angry? And why has your countenance fallen? If you do well, will you not be accepted? And if you do not do well, sin lies at the door. And it's desire is for you, but you should rule over it.'" In other words, Cain could get it right, but it was his choice.

If God was *always* in control, we would be puppets. God gave us a free will. We have to make the right choices, according to what the Word of God tells us. The Bible is our instruction manual. God will take control of our lives if we *ask* and then *allow* Him to do it.

Have you asked God to be the Lord of your life?

Father God, I thank You that You have given us choices. I pray that You will help me to make good ones. Thank You for being the Lord of my life. Amen

# 29

## Well Done

Well done good and faithful servant. Enter into the joy of your Lord.

—Matthew 25:21(NKJV)

Please read Ephesians 6:10–18 (NKJV).

I sit in my sunroom every morning and have my coffee with God. Today the sun is shining, and it is a beautiful morning. I live in a condo next to a golf course, and just beyond my property line is a small heart-shaped pond. Beyond that is one of the greens of the golf course. As I am enjoying the beauty and quiet of God's creation, suddenly there is an invasion of golf carts going in all directions! There must be some sort of special event today. I don't play golf, but it made me think about how the game is played in comparison to how we live our lives. The golfer hits a little white ball, then chases it, only to hit it more and try to get it into a small hole in the ground. The winner is the one who hits the ball the *fewest* amount of times. Hmm, interesting.

Well, for whatever reason, it made me think of the way Satan chases us through life. The more he can make us fall, the more he likes it. In 1 Peter 5:8 (NKJV), it says, "Be sober, be vigilant, because your adversary the devil walks about like a roaring lion, seeking whom he may devour."

Every day we need to resist Satan, and we need to put on our armor—*every day*—to be part of God's Army. In so doing, we are less likely to fall. Our goal in life should be to trust God daily, so when our lives here on earth are finished, we have a low number of falls. When we do fall, if we trust God, He will pick us up, forgive us when we ask, and head us in the right direction—so we will finish well.

As Satan is chasing us, we should be chasing God. When we put on our armor that it talks about in Ephesians 6:10–20 (NKJV), every part of us is covered—except our backs, because God *always* has our backs if we have accepted Jesus as our savior. I want to finish well! I want to hear my Lord say to me when my life on earth is done, "Well done good and faithful servant, enter into the joy of your Lord" (Matthew 25:21 NKJV).

Will you finish well?

Father, please help us put on our armor daily and follow You so that someday we will hear you say "well done." Amen.

# 30

## Encircled

As I look out the airplane window, I see shades of blue as far as the eye can see, and the sky is dotted and streaked with white clouds. Occasionally I see what appear to be islands of various sizes, and encircling them are shades of aqua, turquoise, and green. It is very difficult to see where the sky stops and the sea begins. The puffy white clouds are casting shadows on the water below, the sun is bright, and the water looks very calm with not even a whitecap. How awesome is our God to have made all this beauty for us to enjoy?

This breathtaking scene reminds me of the first chapter of Genesis where the Bible talks about how God made the heavens and the earth—the history of creation. I look down at the beauty of the islands from the view in the airplane and how the sea encircles them, embracing them in beautiful colors. It is a picture of how God's love encircles and embraces us *forever* because "God is love" (1 John 4:8 NKJV).

Psalm 100:5 (NIV) says, "For the Lord is good and His love endures forever. His faithfulness continues through all generations." I certainly want to feel God's love encircling me and feel His ceaseless embrace. Nothing could be more reassuring and comforting.

In Romans 5:8 (NKJV), the Bible says, "But God demonstrates His own love toward us, in that while we were still sinners, Christ died for us." Beloved, that is how much you are loved by our amazingly *awesome God!* I want a relationship with this *awesome God* and to know that He loves me! Don't you?

Lord, thank You for Your unconditional love and for the beauty You have given us here on earth to enjoy. Amen.

# 31

## Potholes

Please read Romans 6: 20–23 (NKJV).

I have been doing short-term mission trips to Jamaica since 2004. It is a beautiful country, and most of the people are welcoming, very polite, and loving. When traveling on the main coastal highway, the scenery is breathtakingly beautiful and the roads are good. However, when you turn off the coastal highway and head up into the mountains where our mission guesthouse is, the roads are full of potholes, so we swerve to try to avoid them.

Sin in our lives is like those potholes; it needs to be avoided. One of the ways we can do that is to read the Bible every day. I love this quote by Dwight L. Moody: "Sin will keep you from the Bible, and the Bible will keep you from sin." Psalm 119:11 (NKJV) says, "Your word have I hidden in my heart, that I might not sin against you."

Satan wants us to fall into these potholes of life. Not all of them can be avoided, *but* we don't have to stay there! In Romans 6:20–23 (NKJV), it tells us we have been set free from sin because of the sacrifice Jesus made for us. We do not have to be stuck in potholes or in sin because Jesus has given us a way out. That is what Paul is telling us in Romans 6:23 (NKJV): "The wages of sin is death, but the gift of God is eternal life in Christ Jesus our Lord."

Will you allow Jesus to lift you from the potholes in your life?

Lord, please help me avoid the potholes of life, but when I can't, please forgive me of my sins and help me return to You. Amen.

# 32

## Seasons

Everything has its Time.

—Ecclesiastes 3: (NKJV)

Please read Ecclesiastes 3:1–8 (NKJV).

I truly enjoy the changing of the seasons where I live and how each one is special in a different way. Spring is my favorite because the beauty of nature comes alive after being asleep for the winter. I enjoy summer and being in the warmth of the sun and maybe even on a beach. Autumn has a wonderful fragrance in the air and gives us one last burst of color before winter. Winter brings cold, crisp air and the beauty of sparkling white snow blanketing the countryside.

Much like the seasons of nature, God tells us in Ecclesiastes 3:1–8 (NKJV) that there are seasons in life. No season, whether in nature or our lives, is without storms. A spring thunderstorm or a winter blizzard in nature and in our lives the loss of a job or loved one, but through it all, God is always there to guide and to comfort us.

In 2 Corinthians 1:3–4 (NKJV), Paul tells us:

> Blessed be the God and Father of our Lord Jesus Christ, the Father of mercies and God of all comfort, who comforts us in all our tribulation,

that we may be able to comfort those who are in any trouble, with the comfort with which we ourselves are comforted by God.

God comforts us in our times of trouble so we can take these wonderful gifts and give them to others in their times of need. When we are willing to do that for others, we show our faith and willingness to love God's people like He loves us through every season of our lives.

Who can you comfort today because of the comfort God has given you?

Father, thank You for Your comfort. You are always there in my times of need, and for that I am very grateful. Amen.

# 33

## Peace

I did a fun research on the word *peace,* and I would recommend
that you do also. I think you will find it very interesting. It basically
means tranquility, quiet, harmony, plus a whole lot more. The
project was enlightening.

In today's world, do you think peace is realistic? There are so many
negative things going on in the world like war; needless killing in
public places such as schools, movie theaters, and malls; attacks of
terrorism; problems in relationships; stress in the work place; and the
list goes on. Will we ever really feel peace?

According to what Jesus tells us in John 14:27, we can. This is Jesus's
personal guarantee of peace. If we truly believe Jesus is in control
for those who have accepted Him as their personal savior and asked
Him to guide and direct their lives, then the answer should be "yes."

We try every way possible to get peace. It cannot be found in
worldly things … *only* in Christ. He gave us the Holy Spirit as a
helper because there are peace stealers everywhere. In Matthew

8:23–27(NKJV), Jesus is asleep in a boat while a storm is raging, but Father God protected Him. God will take care of us. Psalm 46:1 (NKJV) says, "God is our refuge and strength, a very present help in trouble."

We should not be divided between the world and God. Instead, we should trust God, trust His nature, and trust His promises. If He brings you to it, He will bring you through it and give you peace.

Isaiah 26:3 (NKJV) says, "You will keep him in perfect peace, whose mind is stayed on You, because he trusts in You." Let us ask God to give us *His* peace. Be comforted by what Jesus says in John 16:33 (NKJV): "These things I have spoken to you, that in Me you may have peace. In the world you will have tribulation; but be of good cheer, I have overcome the world."

Are you enjoying the peace of God?

Father, we thank You that not only do You give us peace, but You give us *Your* peace. Amen/

# 34

## Angels

I am intrigued by the thought of angels. I often wonder what we would see if we could see them. How many are there, what do they look like, and what are their jobs? There are reasons why God does not allow us to see into the spiritual world, however, He does allow the angels to be seen on occasion. The Bible speaks often of angels because they are God's messengers. In Genesis 19:1 (NKJV), two angels were sent to Sodom to destroy the city. Lot was sitting at the city gate, and God allowed him to see the angels before the city was destroyed. Psalm 91 talks about the safety of abiding in the presence of God. Verse 11 (TPT) says, "God sends angels with special orders to protect you wherever you go, defending you from all harm." (I suggest you read the whole chapter. This is my favorite psalm, and I love this version of the Bible.) I don't know about you, but that gives me comfort!

Probably the passage we are all most familiar with is in Luke 2:8–13 (NKJV) where the shepherds were in the fields watching over their sheep at night. Then in Luke 2:9–10 (NKJV), it says, "And behold, an angel of the Lord stood before them, and the glory of the Lord shone around them, and they were greatly afraid. Then the angel said to them, 'Do not be afraid for behold, I bring you good tidings of great joy, which will be to all people!'" This is when the angels announced the birth of Christ. Why did the angels appear to the shepherds, and how did the shepherds react to the announcement? The story didn't stop there! Can you imagine the next scene? Luke 2:13–14 (NKJV) says, "And suddenly there was with the angel a *multitude* of the heavenly host praising God and saying, 'Glory to God in the highest, and on earth peace, and good will toward men.'" What an amazingly breathtaking picture, and maybe even a small glimpse of what heaven will be like.

In Hebrews 13:2 (NKJV), the Bible tells us, "Do not forget to entertain strangers for by so doing some have unwittingly entertained angels." There is no doubt that angels are real and that they seem to be busy doing God's work and praising Him. They are another example to us of how we should be God's messengers, spreading the good news of the gospel of Christ and praising God.

Will you take time to praise God today?

Father, we thank You for Your Angels, even though we're not able to see them. We know they are Your messengers and they are real because Your Word tells us they are. Amen.

# 35

# Whiter than Snow

Wash me, and I shall be whiter than snow.
—Psalm 51:7 (NKJV)

As I look out my window on this cold, windy, and snowy winter day, the earth is covered with a blanket of pure white snow. It brings to mind the above scripture in Psalms. In Isaiah 1:18 (NKJV), the Bible says, "'Come now, and let us reason together,' says the Lord. 'Though your sins are like scarlet, they shall be white as snow; though they are red like crimson, they shall be as wool.'" This is an invitation from God to repentance. God will pardon our sins, no matter what they are, if we truly repent and turn to Him. He can forgive us because of what Christ did on the cross—He died for us *all*, and the blood He shed for us covers our sins, cleanses us, and makes us whiter than snow.

I cannot imagine anything whiter than snow. Sometimes, in the right light, snow looks as though it has been sprinkled with diamond dust. I am sure of one thing, if God says it in His Word, the Bible, I believe it, even if it is beyond my imagination.

There is another side to this if you go on to read Isaiah 1:19 (NKJV), which gives us this promise: "If you are willing and obedient, you shall eat the good of the land." We always have a choice, to choose Him or not. However, there are consequences if we do not. Then He says in Isaiah 1:20 (NKJV), "But if you refuse and rebel, you shall be devoured by the sword"; for the mouth of the Lord has spoken." You might argue this was a long time ago and not meant for us today. The Bible says in John 10:30 (NKJV), "I and my Father are one." Then in Hebrews 13:8 (NKJV), it says, "Jesus Christ is the same yesterday, today, and forever." The choice is always ours. God is sovereign and good and wants the best for all of His children, but the choice is ours.

Will you repent and let God wash you and make you whiter than snow?

Father, we thank You for Your Word and for loving us so much. Please wash our sins away and make us whiter than snow, in Jesus's name. Amen.

# 36

## Abide

I am the vine and you are the branches. He who abides in Me, and I in him, bears much fruit; for without Me, you can do nothing.

—John 15:5 (NKJV)

Please read John 15: 1–8 (NKJV).

Looking out my window this morning, enjoying the beauty of a snowy winter day, I saw a little bird perched on the branch of a bush. The wind is blowing, and it is snowing and very cold. The little bird was all puffed up—to stay warm, I suppose—and trying desperately to stay on the branch, despite the wind.

The scene above brought to mind the scripture in John 15:5 (NKJV). I wonder, do I try as desperately to abide in my Lord? Some other words to explain abide are: endure, withstand, and accept.

Jesus says that without Him, we can do nothing. He goes on to say in verse 6 of John 15 (NKJV) that the branches will be cast out and thrown into the fire to be burned. If the branch does not "abide" in the vine, it dies. John 15:7 (NKJV) says, "If you abide in Me, and My words abide in you, you will ask what you desire, and it shall be done for you." What an amazing promise! There are powerful words in these verses about the depth of our relationships with God. Will you try desperately to abide in and hold on to Jesus, like the little bird tried to hold on to the branch? If you will, John 15:8 (NKJV) says, "By this My Father is glorified, that you bear much fruit; so you will be My disciples."

Will you abide in Jesus? Will you be His disciple?

Lord, thank You for Your Word. Please help me to abide, be Your disciple, and glorify You with my life. Amen.

# 37

## Grace

And He said to me, "My grace is sufficient for you, for My strength is made perfect in weakness." Therefore, most gladly I will rather boast in my infirmities, that the power of Christ may rest upon me.

—2 Corinthians 12:9 (NKJV)

The word *grace* is used over 160 times in the Bible, and the previous verse is my favorite of those. Grace means the unmerited favor of God. We do not deserve it, but it is a free gift from God. In 2 Corinthians 12:9 (NKJV), Paul is saying that through Paul's own weaknesses and by God's grace, Christ's power in him is made more evident to others. That is also true of us today.

Another meaning for grace is to show great favor. God's grace is given *to* us because of His love *for* us. God's love is extravagant—He loves us unconditionally. God is both willing and able to give us unconditional love. The word for that kind of love is *agape*. There is nothing you can do to make God love you more or less. What kind of relationship are you having with God? The free gift of a relationship with God is called *grace*. Grace shows that God loves us, and He wants us all to respond. Jesus says, "Come to me all you who labor and are heavy laden, and I will give you rest" (Matthew 11:28 NKJV). This is a request from Jesus because of His love for us. Saying yes to Jesus is new life. There is nothing that the world can give that Jesus doesn't already offer.

Where are you right now? What is God saying to you? Will you accept His gift of grace?

Lord, thank You for Your grace. Help us not only to receive it but also to extend it to others. Amen.

# 38

## Hope

> I will come forth as gold.
>
> —Job 23:10 (NKJV)

Please read Job 23:1–12 (NKJV)

Are you feeling stressed by the busyness of life? Are you going through a difficult time, maybe even a tragedy in your life? Take heart, dear one; God is watching over you, even if you feel He is far from you. Job felt that way too in some of the verses in this passage. Our God is a God of *hope!* Romans 15:13 (NKJV) says, "Now may the God of hope fill you with all joy and peace in believing, that you may abound in hope by the power of the Holy Spirit." God does not want you just to *have hope* but to *abound in hope.* The general meaning of abound is to have a large amount of something.

As followers of Christ, hope should be a vital part of who we are. Hope, to believers, means that we rely on the faithfulness and goodness of God in every situation. In Ephesians 2:12–13 (NKJV), the Bible says:

> That at that time, you were without Christ, being aliens from the commonwealth of Israel and strangers from the covenants of promise, having no hope and without God in the world. But now in

Christ Jesus you who once were far off have been brought near by the blood of Christ.

God is the source of hope for all believers.

Will you let Him be your hope?

Father God, we thank You for the hope that You give us through Jesus Christ, our Lord. Amen.

# 39

## Celebrate

"For I know the plans I have for you," declares the Lord, "plans to prosper you and not to harm you, plans to give you hope and a future. Then you will call on me and come and pray to me, and I will listen to you. You will seek me and find me when you seek me with all your heart."

—Jeremiah 29:11–13 (NIV)

We have many holidays and special occasions we like to celebrate, and rightfully so: Christmas, the birth of Jesus; Easter, the death, burial, and glorious resurrection of our Savior; and New Year's Day, the beginning of a New Year and many new adventures. On a more personal level, we celebrate weddings, anniversaries, birthdays, graduations, and many, many more.

I believe God wants us to enjoy our lives, and He made each of us unique and special. In Psalm 139:14 (NKJV), the Bible says, "I will praise you, for I am fearfully and wonderfully made; marvelous are Your works, and that my soul knows very well." We are each a masterpiece of God. That is something to celebrate! And to think, we are made in God's image. In Genesis 1:27 (NKJV), the Bible says, "So God created man in His own image; in the image of God He created him; male and female He created them." I guess the question has always been *why?* Why were we created? Each one of us needs to personally seek the answer to that question. We need to seek God to find out the answer because I believe He has a purpose for each one of us. In the previous verses, the Bible talks about how God has a plan for each of us and that when we seek Him with all our heart, He *will* be found. Now *that* is something to celebrate!

Are you seeking God with all your heart?

Lord, thank You for my life. Help me to seek You to discover my purpose. Amen.

# 40

## The Potter

Yet You, Lord, are our Father. We are the clay, You are the potter; we are all the work of your hand.
—Isaiah 64:8 (NIV)

I have friends in Jamaica who own a pottery shop and are gifted potters. They are called the Clonmel Potters. Clonmel is the area where they live and have their shop. I so enjoy being in their workshop and watching Donald take the clay, throw it onto the potter's wheel, and begin to make the wheel move with his feet. As the wheel rotates, he uses his hands to shape the clay, adding a little water when necessary. He is very careful and precise in how he uses his hands to shape the wet clay. When the wheel stops and he is finished, he has created something very beautiful.

That is what we are to God; we are like clay that He wants to shape and make into a beautiful vessel to be used. When the potter is finished shaping the clay on the wheel, that is only the beginning. The vessel must dry, then needs to be fired at a very high heat to make it strong so it can be used. Also, glaze needs to be applied to give it color and beauty. As we seek God and desire to grow as Christians, that is what God does with us. Sometimes because of the tribulations we go through, we feel like we are in the middle of a fire, but our Lord is with us. In Daniel 3:19–30 (NKJV), the Bible talks about Shadrach, Meshach, and Abed-Nego being thrown into the fiery furnace, but "the hair of their head was not singed nor were their garments affected, and the smell of fire was not on them" (Daniel 3:27 NKJV). That was because Jesus was with them. They came out better and stronger than they were when they went into the furnace.

Without the potter, clay is just dirt! Without God and His Word, we cannot be made into what He wants us to be. He wants each one of us to become a living vessel to be used to glorify Him and to love His people.

Will you allow God to be the potter in your life, to mold you into something beautiful for Him?

Father, please mold me into the person You created me to be. Amen.

*Donald Johnson of the Clonmel Potters*

# 41

## Rain

And now why are you waiting? Arise and be baptized, and wash away your sins, calling on the name of the Lord.

—Acts 22:16 (NKJV)

I am watching it rain and looking at how the rain makes things outside shine and look clean. That is what happens to us when we give our lives to Christ and accept Him as our personal savior. He washes away our sins, and we become new.

In 1 Corinthians 5:17 (NKJV), the Bible says, "Therefore if anyone is in Christ, he is a new creation, old things have passed away, behold, all things have become new." That is what God wants for each one of us, and that is why Jesus died on the cross. We can all be forgiven of our sins and become new so that when we die, we will live with Him for eternity in heaven.

We should begin to read and study the Bible because it helps us learn about Jesus and how He wants us to live our lives. The Bible is our instruction manual for life. Titus 3:4–6 (NIV) says:

> But when the kindness and love of God our Savior appeared, he saved us, not because of righteous things we had done, but because of His mercy.

He saved us through the washing of rebirth and renewal by the Holy Spirit, whom he poured out on us generously through Jesus Christ our Savior.

In Romans 10:9 (NIV), it says "that if you confess with your mouth, 'Jesus is Lord,' and believe in your heart that God raised him from the dead, you will be saved."

When Jesus was baptized by John the Baptist, it was a picture of His death, burial, and resurrection. That is what happens when we are baptized, our sins are washed away, and we are made new in Christ.

This can be the first day of a new life for you if you have not already accepted Jesus as your personal savior. Will you accept Jesus today?

Father, we thank You for the water that washes us clean and makes us new. It is a picture of what Jesus did for us, and we are grateful. Amen.

# 42

## Heaven

Have you ever wondered what heaven is like? I certainly have. From what the Bible tells us, it is a place of magnificent beauty. The gates where we enter are made of pearls, and the streets we will walk on are made of gold, so pure it will be unlike any we have ever seen.

The Bible talks about a *third heaven* in 2 Corinthians 12:2 (NKJV) and in 2 Corinthians 12:4, that it is "paradise." When Jesus was on the cross in Luke 23:43, He said this to one of the criminals, hanging beside him on a cross: "And Jesus said to him, 'Assuredly, I say to you, today you will be with me in Paradise'" (NKJV). In a sermon I heard many years ago, the pastor told us there are three heavens. The first heaven is the one we see during the day—blue sky, clouds, and sunshine. The second heaven is the one we see at night—darkness, the moon, and the stars. The third heaven we cannot see, but that is where God lives. That is very exciting to think about. At least it is for me.

Philippians 3:20 (NKJV) says, "For our citizenship is in heaven." If we belong to Jesus, we are not citizens of this world; we are only passing through. That is a comforting thought. This is Satan's world, which is fairly evident. As we look at everything that is going on in the world today, it is getting worse as time goes on. Satan is a fallen angel who was cast out of heaven to earth, and one-third of the angels followed him—but, be encouraged by Jesus's words in John 14:1–3 (NKJV):

> Let not your heart be troubled; you believe in God, believe also in Me. In My Father's house are many mansions; if it were not so, I would have told you. I go to prepare a place for you. And if I go and prepare a place for you, I will come again and receive you to Myself; that where I am, there you may be also.

Lord Jesus, thank You for the hope that comes with the thought of heaven and living with You for eternity. Thank You that You love us so much. Amen.

# 43

## Awesome

What does the word *awesome* mean to you? In society today, a lot
of people seem to think a lot of things are *awesome* because you
frequently hear the word. "That is an awesome outfit." "What an
awesome dessert!" "What an awesome car!" Even if we do something
nice, it is not just nice anymore—it is "awesome."

In the Bible, Psalm 68:35 (NKJV) says, "O, God, You are more
awesome than your holy places. The God of Israel is He who gives
strength and power to His people. Blessed be God."

When I think about God and finding words to describe Him,
*awesome* is my number one choice. That is what Job says in Job 37:22
(NKJV): "He comes from the north as golden splendor; With God is
awesome majesty." There just are not enough words to describe God
and what He means to us, but what Job said was excellent.

Sometimes I use the Nelson's NKJV Study Bible. In the concordance
in the back, there are thirty-three references to the word "awesome."
They are all in the Old Testament, and most are in direct reference
to God. The word awesome means "impressive" or "excellent,"

which certainly describes our God! A lot of words have more than one meaning, so they can be used differently. When using the word awesome, I choose to use it to describe my "awesome and majestic God."

How will you use the word *awesome* today?

Father God, we thank You for words and pray You will help us to always use them in a positive way—to encourage, empower, and bring honor to You. Amen.

# 44

## Temptation

No temptation has overtaken you except such as is common to man; but God is faithful, who will not allow you to be tempted beyond what you are able, but with the temptation will also make the way of escape, that you may be able to bear it.
—1 Corinthians 10:13 (NKJV)

Temptation is a very difficult thing, but it only becomes sin when we act on it. The best way to keep temptation from turning into sin is to walk away, flee, run! Temptations are a part of life and have been since the beginning of time. God loves us so much that all we have to do is ask, and He will give us the strength to endure.

There is a very good example in the Bible in Genesis 39:1–12 (NKJV). Joseph had been taken to Egypt. In Genesis 39:2 (NKJV), it says, "The Lord was with Joseph, and he was a successful man." Joseph lived and worked in Potiphar's house. Potiphar, who was an officer of Pharaoh, recognized that Joseph was successful because God was with him, so he put him in charge of his whole household—everything. Joseph was a faithful servant. He was forced into a foreign country because of the anger and jealousy of his brothers. Joseph remained faithful to God, and God continued to bless him—even in the household where he was a servant. In verse 6 of Genesis 39, the Bible says, "Now Joseph was handsome in form and appearance" (NKJV).

It wasn't long until Potiphar's wife noticed Joseph and began to flirt with him, but Joseph resisted, and Potiphar's wife did not give up. Because of the presence of God in Joseph's life, he was able to resist temptation. In Genesis 39:12 (NKJV), we read "that she caught him by his garment, saying 'Lie with me,' but he left his garment in her hand, and fled outside." That is strength of character and willpower that only God can give. That is what He did for Joseph. It makes me think of the scripture in Philippians 4:13 (NIV): "I can do all things through Him who gives me strength." Joseph was a strong man of God who wanted to do what was right. He loved God and did not want to sin against Him. Read 1 Corinthians 10:13 (NKJV) again. God will always give us a way out, as long as we trust Him and stay focused on Him.

Will you trust God today when you are tempted?

Lord, thank You for always being there in every situation and giving us guidance and strength to flee when temptations arise. Amen.

# 45

## Forgiveness

Then Peter came to Him and said, "Lord, how often shall my brother sin against me, and I forgive him? Up to seven times?" Jesus said to him, "I do not say to you up to seven times, but up to seventy times seven."

—Matthew 18:21–22 (NJKV)

What is Jesus really saying to Peter? Is there a limit to the number of times we are to forgive? I don't believe that is what Jesus means. I believe Jesus means that no matter how often we are sinned against, we must *always* forgive. If you choose not to forgive, that sin festers in your own heart and soul. So who is it really hurting? The one who chooses *not* to forgive. Matthew 6:15 (TPT) says, "But if you withhold forgiveness from others, your Father withholds forgiveness from you." This is Jesus speaking to us!

Bitterness poisons the spirit, and the results can be horrific. If we refuse to let go of a wrong we have suffered, it is like being locked into a prison of our own making. Then bitterness, anger, and resentment are in there with us. The results can be devastating—a friendship ruined, a family divided, or a marriage destroyed. The list of tragedies that could happen is endless, plus Satan loves every minute of it!

In Ephesians 1:7 (NKJV), Paul writes, "In Him we have redemption through His blood, the forgiveness of sins, according to the riches of His grace." Jesus died on the cross so our sins could be forgiven. He paid the ultimate price for us, who are sinners, when He was perfect and without sin. If Jesus could do that for us, then we surely should forgive others.

Is there someone you need to forgive today?

Lord, thank You for dying for me and my sins and forgiving me. Please help me to forgive others like You forgive me. Amen.

# 46

## Blessed

Jesus said to him, "Thomas, because you have seen
Me, you have believed. Blessed are those who have
not seen and yet have believed."

—John 20:29 (NKJV)

What do you think about when you hear the word *blessed*? It can
also be pronounced *bles-id* and *blest* and has several meanings. My
favorite is "divinely favored." We talk about being blessed in so many
ways, and it is different for each one of us.

I was with a friend recently. During our conversation, I made the
statement, "I am so blessed." She asked me if I had ever looked up
the meaning of the word blessed and suggested that I should. She
had just done that and found it very interesting. So I did. I would
like to suggest you do the same because I think you will be surprised
by what you find.

I love what Jesus said in the previous verse. He was saying to Thomas,
"It is easier to believe in Him when you see Him for yourself, *but* for
those who have not seen Him and believe, that is a special blessing."
When Jesus says, "those who have not seen," He is talking about all
who have believed in Him since the ascension to the Father (John
20:29 NKJV). (Please read 1 Peter 1:8–9 NKJV.) I also love the

passage in Matthew 5:1–16 (NKJV) known as the Beatitudes or the Sermon on the Mount. Jesus uses the word blessed numerous times.

I love words and learning something new about a word I have known and used for a long time. My favorite words are found in the Bible—God's Word. We can read, read, and reread and always learn something new because God's Word is alive! I am truly *blessed* to have a Bible, God's Word.

How do you feel about the word *blessed* today?

Thank You, Father, for blessing us, Your sons and daughters, and showing us favor today. Amen.

# 47

## New Life

Therefore, if anyone is in Christ, he is a new creation; old things have passed away and all things have become new.

—2 Corinthians 5:17 (NKJV)

I start my mornings by having coffee with God, and when I can, I do that in my sunroom. It is a beautiful spring morning. The trees are beginning to wake up and turn green after a long winter of being asleep. In my front yard is a tree that is totally pink with little flowers, but if you look really closely, you can see green leaves beginning to peek through. The sky is blue with a few white clouds, and the sun shining on the grass makes the dew sparkle like diamonds. Spring is my favorite season because the earth comes back to life and there is much beauty to behold. It is a picture of new life. It makes me think of the scripture above. This scripture means when you give yourself to Christ and accept Him as your personal savior, your life will change. Instead of living for ourselves, we live for Christ, and as a believer in Christ, we should look at the world through Christ's eyes, putting on our Jesus glasses.

In Colossians 3:8–10 (NKJV), the Bible says:

> But now you yourselves are to put off all these: anger, wrath, malice, blasphemy, filthy language out

of your mouth. Do not lie to one another, since you have put off the old man with his deeds, and have put on the new man who is renewed in knowledge according to the image of Him who created him.

New life—it changes us, if we let it, into who God wants us to be.

Will you allow God to give you new life?

Father, thank You for spring and new life. Help my new life to bring forth glory to You. Amen.

# 48

## Solitude

Now in the morning, having risen a long while before daylight, He went out to a solitary place; and there He prayed.

—Mark 1:35 (NKJV)

I am very much a people person, so thinking about solitude was very foreign to me until my husband passed away. Shortly after that, I retired and I was spending more and more time alone. By that I mean living by myself without another person living with me to share my life with. I am never alone because Hebrews 13:5 (NKJV) in God's Word says, "For He Himself has said, 'I will never leave you nor forsake you.'" Solitude simply means being by yourself with no other living being with you.

In the previous scripture, Mark 1:35 (NKJV), even Jesus practiced solitude. He would go to a solitary place where there were no distractions and pray to His heavenly Father. We were designed for community to spend time together as families, friends, and a church family. In Hebrews 10:24–25 (NKJV), it says:

And let us consider one another in order to stir up love and good works, not forsaking the assembling of ourselves together, as is the manner of some, but

exhorting one another, and so much more as you see
the Day approaching.

There is something special and powerful about seeking solitude from time to time, even daily. When we do that and seek God in our times of solitude, He *will* be found if we seek Him with all our hearts. (Please read Deuteronomy 4:29 NKJV.) That is where we find love, peace, joy, and strength—in the presence of our Lord.

I have found I truly enjoy my times of solitude. That is where God inspires me to write and where I pray and seek Him. It seems to fill me up so I can go out and encourage and love others.

Will you seek God in solitude today and live in the power only He can give you?

Father, please help us to find that quiet place today where there are no distractions so we can seek Your face and find Your will for us. Amen.

# 49

## Spiritual Warfare

And take the helmet of salvation, and the sword of
the Spirit, which is the Word of God.
—Ephesians 6:17 (NKJV)

Whether we believe it or not, we are fighting a spiritual battle every day. If we are believers, Christ followers, we need to arm ourselves against all the attacks of our enemy, Satan. He is not some cartoon character with horns, a pitchfork, and a funny tail! He is real and comes against us in ways we least expect. He is the father of lies and trickery, so we need to learn his ways so we can fight him. God's Word is our only defense.

In the Bible in James 4:6–7 (NKJV), it says, "But He gives more grace. Therefore, He says, God resists the proud, but gives grace to the humble. Therefore, submit to God. Resist the devil and he will flee from you." We can't do it without God! If we think what we do for God doesn't matter, then read 1 Corinthians 3:11–15 (NKJV). This is a promise that what we do for Jesus will last forever! When we read the scriptures, meditate on them, and memorize them, we are preparing for when Satan comes against us, to take a stand against his schemes. In Ephesians 6:10–20 (NKJV), Paul gives us in detail the "Full Armor of God." We need to memorize it to help us prepare to be in God's army. Satan knows his time is short, but we know who wins!

If you haven't chosen Jesus, you have made a choice!

Thank You Father for Your Word and giving us everything we need to fight a good fight for Jesus. Amen.

# 50

## Cast Your Cares

But He gives more grace. Therefore, He says: "God resists the proud but gives grace to the humble."
—James 4:6 (NKJV)

Please read James 4:1–10 (NKJV). These verses talk about how pride promotes strife. James tells us that our behaviors clearly illustrate our beliefs. God cares about our hearts and right motives. God is calling you to sit at His feet and receive love, peace, and power that He freely offers.

In Luke 10:38–42 (NKJV) is the story of Mary and Martha. Jesus was at their house teaching, and Mary was sitting at His feet. Martha was busy serving and was upset because her sister was not helping her. Jesus lovingly said to Martha in Luke 10:42 (NKJV), "But one thing is needed, and Mary has chosen that good part, which will not be taken away from her." That does not mean serving is not good or needed, because it is, but rather we need the love, peace, and power we receive from sitting at Christ's feet so we can then go and serve.

Satan does *not* want us reading and studying the Bible and learning from God's Word because he cannot be where Jesus is. Satan wants us to be *busy, troubled,* and *worldly,* putting more emphasis on things and doing what we want to do. We need to trade the troubles of this world for the peace that only Jesus can give us.

In 1 Peter 5:6–7 (NKJV), the Bibles says, "Therefore, humble yourselves under the mighty hand of God, that He may exalt you in due time, casting all your care upon Him, for He cares for you." He wants to love you and give you peace and power to serve Him.

Will you take time to sit at Jesus's feet today?

Lord, please help me today to make time for You and cast all my cares on You. Amen.

# 51

# Assurance

Have you ever doubted your salvation? Have you maybe done or said something that makes you wonder, "Am I really saved and going to heaven?" According to the previous verse, there is assurance for those "who believe in the name of the Son of God" (1 John 5:13 NIV). It says, "I write these things" (1 John 5:13 NIV)—so maybe we should go back to the beginning of the chapter to see what is being referred to. Please read 1 John 5:1–13 (NIV).

In 1 John 5:4 (NIV) it says, "For everyone born of God overcomes the world. This is the victory that has overcome the world, even our faith." The faith that this verse is talking about is faith in Jesus Christ, the Son of God, who died for us. He obeys God, and if we love God, we will want to obey Him and find pleasure in doing so. In 1 John 5:12 (NIV), John says, "Whoever has the Son has life; whoever does not have the Son of God does not have life." It seems so simple! John is clearly saying our relationship with the Son determines whether or not we possess eternal life. Simple, yet profound! John is telling us that if we have accepted Jesus as our personal savior and believe, we have assurance of eternal life.

Do you have that assurance?

Thank You, Father, for Your Word, which gives us knowledge, understanding, and assurance of our eternity in heaven with You. Amen

# 52

## Serving

How are you serving our amazing and awesome God? Once we have accepted Jesus as our personal savior and the Holy Spirit lives in us, we are each given a spiritual gift. We are to use that gift to further the kingdom by serving Christ here on earth, loving our brothers and sisters in Christ, and sharing the gospel. In Ephesians 4:11–12 (NKJV), Paul says, "And He Himself gave some to be apostles, some prophets, some evangelists, and some pastors and teachers, for the equipping of the saints for the work of ministry, for the edifying of the body of Christ."

You may be thinking you do not have any spiritual gifts to use to serve Christ, but you do! That is one of the reasons we need to read the Bible and pray every day—so we can serve Him. We need to search the scriptures to learn and become all that God wants us to be and to know God and His heart for His people. There are many spiritual gifts—gifts of prophecy, ministry, teaching, encouraging, giving, leadership, and mercy are just a few. (Please read Romans 12:6–8 NKJV.) Spiritual gifts are given to every believer. We all receive different gifts, but they all work together, just as the many different parts of the human body work together. Spiritual gifts are given to the body of Christ so that we can serve as one for effective ministry. When you find your spiritual gift, you will develop it to serve God by serving others. In Mark 10:45 (NKJV), the Bible says, "For even the Son of Man did not come to be served, but to serve, and to give His life as a ransom for many."

How will you serve God?

Father, please open our eyes of understanding and show each of us our gift so that we may see the person You want us to be and serve You by serving others. Amen.

# 53

## Living Water

Jesus answered her, "If you knew the gift of God and who it is that asks you for a drink, you would have asked him and he would have given you living water."

—John 4:10 (NIV)

As I look at the golf course next to where I live, there are sprinklers watering the green that is just across a small pond. Everything is becoming very dry, and there are a lot of patches of brown grass. We need rain! It has not rained for a while now, and that wonderful rain from heaven is what waters the earth to make things grow and keep the grass green.

That is what Jesus is to us: living water. Without Him, we are dead in our sins, but when we accept Him as our personal savior, He is our living water. In the previous scripture, the Samaritan woman did not understand the spiritual message because she was thinking about the physical water. How could Jesus provide water without a way to draw it from the well? In John 4:14 (NKJV), Jesus says, "But whoever drinks of the water that I shall give him will never thirst. But the water that I shall give him will become in him a fountain of water springing up into everlasting life."

A fountain is certainly different from a well because it does not require manual labor to receive the water. The gift that Jesus gives, "A fountain of water springing up into everlasting life," suggests the divine life for all believers (John 4:14 NKJV). Drinking the water Jesus gives us so freely gives us eternal life. The story of Jesus and the Samaritan woman is a good one, full of hope, so please read the whole story. It is found in John 4:5–26 (NKJV).

Lord, thank You for salvation. Thank You for Your Word, which teaches us and gives us hope and for Your living water that sustains us. Amen.

# 54

# Light in Darkness

You are the light of the world. A city that is set on
a hill cannot be hidden.

—Matthew 5:14 (NKJV)

When Jesus walked the earth, He was the light of the world. Since
His return to heaven, His followers are to reflect His light and Glory.
That is what Jesus is saying in the previous scripture. The greatest
thing that we (those who are believers) can hope for is that people
can see Christ *in* us, that we truly reflect God's glory and the love
Christ has for *all* mankind. We may be the only "Jesus" some people
ever see. I once heard a pastor say before his sermon, "Less of me
Lord, and more of You. May they see You through my words." That
is what we, as Christ followers, should be saying as we share Christ's
love with others.

Sometimes people rebel against the light because it exposes flaws
they do not want to see or sin they do not want to change. In Job
24:13 (NKJV), the Bible says, "There are those who rebel against
the light; they do not know its ways nor abide in its path." Satan
will use that, or whatever it takes, to keep people from believing
in Christ. In 2 Corinthians 11:14 (NKJV), the Bible says, "And no
wonder! For Satan himself transforms himself into an angel of light."
He masquerades! His main tool he uses against us is deception. We
must remember that for every good thing God has, Satan has a

counterfeit! In Psalm 119:105 (NKJV), it says, "Your word is a lamp to my feet and a light to my path." We need to stay in the Word daily so we can quench the fiery darts of Satan. (Please read Ephesians 6:16 NKJV.) Then we can become children of light and let God's love shine through us.

In whose darkness will you be a light today?

Lord, please help us to glorify You and bring light to a dark world so that more may come to know You, love You, and serve You. Amen.

# 55

## Simple Pleasures

Then God saw everything that He had made, and indeed it was very good. So the evening and morning were the sixth day.

—Genesis 1:31 (NKJV)

My friend and I were on our way home from a concert in the park in my home town one summer evening when she said in an excited voice to look at the moon. It was just coming up, and it looked huge! It was full and a beautiful soft, pastel orange color. It was almost dark, but we could see that some of the corn in the fields along the country road had begun to tassel. We rolled down our windows so we could smell the sweet summer air, and there were fireflies everywhere! When we were growing up, we called them lightning bugs. I drove slowly so we could enjoy the simple pleasures of an Indiana summer night.

If you read the Creation story in Genesis, chapters 1 and 2 (NKJV), you will find that God created the heavens and the earth and everything on the earth, and then He created man before He rested on the seventh day. What an amazing birthday present for Adam! Then Adam was given the privilege of naming the animals. What an awesome experience that must have been!

God wants us to enjoy what He has given us; however, it comes with a command. In 1 Timothy 6:17–19 (NIV), God's Word says:

> Command those who are rich in this present age not to be haughty, nor to trust in uncertain riches but in the living God, who gives us richly all things to enjoy. Let them do good, that they be rich in good works, ready to give, willing to share, storing up for themselves a good foundation for the time to come, that they may lay hold on eternal life.

Paul is instructing Timothy to tell the wealthy to trust in God and not in their wealth. They are to remember God is the one who gave them their wealth, so they are to be generous. We are to enjoy what God has so generously given us, but we are also to use it to bless others and further God's kingdom. Wealth and riches are *not* to be used for selfish living.

There are many simple pleasures God has given us all to enjoy. May we always remember to thank Him for each and every blessing.

Lord, help us to enjoy all that You have so graciously and generously given to us and to remember to thank You. Please help us to use the blessings You have poured out on us to also bless others for Your glory. Amen.

# 56

## Nature

For since the Creation of the world His invisible attributes are clearly seen, being understood by the things that are made, even His eternal power and Godhead, so that they are without excuse.

—Romans 1:20 (NKJV)

Have you ever laid down in the cool, green grass and looked up at the blue sky, looking at lots of white, puffy clouds? Then did you watch the clouds move and wonder what else is out there? As the cool breeze rushes over your body, you look at the clouds and find the shape of a cat, or an ice cream cone, or an angel, and wonder, *How far away are they, and how fast is the earth spinning?* What an amazing world we live in! We are truly blessed. I have thought for a very long time that God's favorite colors must be blue and green because there is so much of those colors in nature—the sky and water and the grass and trees. I have also wondered how people can look at all of this—nature—and not believe there is an almighty God!

In the previous scripture, Paul is saying that when looking at nature, we *should* see God, its creator. If you look at flowers, birds, mountains, a storm, or humans, you should see God's power and wisdom. Even though we cannot see God, the evidence of His eternal power can be seen clearly by truly looking at and studying nature.

Furthermore, there are *no excuses* for not seeing Him through His creation, according to Romans 1:20 (NKJV). My friends, that scripture is both powerful and profound!

Will you see God today through His awesome creation?

Lord, please help us to always be looking for You because Your Word says that if we do, You *will* be found. Amen.

*Butterfly on coneflower*

# 57

## Seek Him

And you will seek Me and find Me, when you search for me with all your heart.
—Jeremiah 29:13 (NKJV)

I don't know about you, but I love birds. Watching them always makes me smile, especially when it is one you don't see often, like a bluebird. I have had the pleasure of seeing a bluebird quite often this summer, and it always makes me smile. This morning, I was sitting in my sunroom, doing my devotions, when a bluebird came to the window and looked in at me as if to say, "Good morning," then it flew away. I was excited to see it up close and personal! Its bright blue feathers, rusty chest, and white belly were brilliant and beautiful.

Do you suppose that is how God sees us when we say a quick prayer or do a two- or three-minute devotion before flying off for our busy day? I think He smiles when we seek Him, but it saddens Him when we leave, especially if we only spend a few minutes with Him. I think He wants quality time with us, to love us, comfort us, and teach us, and that takes more than a few minutes a day. He promises to always be there for us, to never leave us (please read Hebrews 13:5 NKJV), but He wants us to seek Him and be intentional about the time we spend with Him. In Jeremiah 29:13 (NKJV), Jesus says,

"And you will seek Me and find Me, when you search for me with all your heart."

Will you seek the Lord today and make Him smile?

Lord, please help us be more intentional about spending time with You today and every day. Amen.

# 58

## Cleansing

That He might sanctify and cleanse her with the washing of water by the word.
—Ephesians 5:26 (NKJV)

I enjoy watching the rain as it falls on the pond behind my house, how it causes little rings and ripples and cleans the nastiness from the top of the pond, bringing out its beauty once again. I like hearing the sound of the rain as it falls on the roof and the way the air smells, fresh and clean. Rain waters the earth and makes it beautiful. The birds are even chirping, enjoying the summer shower.

In Ephesians 5:26 (NKJV), "by the word" means that Christ has declared the church to be His own. Paul is giving us a picture of baptism—the baptism of the church—cleansing, sanctifying, and consecrating the whole church.

After we accept Jesus as our personal savior, we are then baptized. This is a picture of us as we die to our old life, our sins being washed away, and rise to a new life in Christ. The nastiness is washed away, and we are made beautiful again.

These are pictures of water as being cleansing, making us clean and new in order to live a life for Christ. Jesus died on the cross, shed

His blood for the remission of sins, was buried, then rose from the grave on the third day. Jesus died for *you!*

Will you live for Jesus?

Father, thank You for sending Jesus to earth to live as an example for us then die a cruel death for us because of Your love for us. Help me now to live for Jesus and to bring glory and honor to You. Amen.

# 59

## Sorrow

I have overcome the world.

—John 16:33 (NKJV)

Have you ever had so much sorrow in your life that you wanted to run away, hide, and be by yourself? I have! I think most of us have been in that situation at one time or another. I remember a pastor saying that, on average, we face two crises every year. If you are not facing one now, you probably will soon. Wow! That is not a good thought!

Recently, our family had two deaths in the same week, and the following week another family member went to the ER and another had a very serious surgery.

What we *always* need to remember is that no matter what our circumstances, God is there! His children are His delight! In Zephaniah 3:17 (NKJV), the Bible says, "The Lord your God in your midst, The Mighty One, will save; He will rejoice over you with His love, He will rejoice over you with singing."

We live in a fallen world, but Jesus says in John 16:33 (NKJV), "These things I have spoken, to you, that in Me you may have peace.

In the world you will have tribulation; but be of good cheer, I have overcome the world."

Are you going through a time of sorrow? Cry out to Jesus!

Lord, please help us and comfort us in our times of sorrow. Let us remember that You are *always* there! Amen.

# 60

## Running on Empty

For this reason, since the day we heard about you, we have not stopped praying for you. We continually ask God to fill you with the knowledge of his will through all the wisdom and understanding that the Spirit gives, so that you may live a life worthy of the Lord and please him in every way: bearing fruit in every good work, growing in the knowledge of God.
—Colossians 1:9–10 (NIV)

Are you tired and do you feel like you are running on empty? Do you feel like you are meeting yourself coming and going? A very long time ago, there was a commercial on TV, and as the man was leaving his house, he was also just coming home! It was funny, but when life gets to be that way, it is anything but funny. It seems as though life continues to become busier and busier. Most often the things that keep us busy are good, but what are they keeping us from? Reading the Bible and praying, family time around the dinner table, or going to a small group Bible study. Are we so busy we have no time for God to fill us up? I have found when I take time to read my Bible, pray, and spend time with God in the morning, my day goes much smoother. When we make God a priority, life is simply better.

In Colossians 1:9–10 (NIV), Paul is praying for the new believers in Colosse, asking God to give them wisdom, knowledge, strength, and joy so they would grow and live in God's will for them. We need understanding in order for that to happen. We need to be studying God's Word and praying so we can find out what His will is for each of us.

Romans 15:13 (NIV) says, "May the God of hope fill you with all joy and peace as you trust in Him, so that you may overflow with hope by the power of the Holy Spirit." Our physical bodies need food for energy and life. Our souls need spiritual food, the Word of God, for growth and life as well.

Will you allow God to fill you up today?

Lord, please help us to make You a priority so we can live in Your will for our lives and share hope with others. Amen.

# 61

## Obedience

Walk in obedience to all that the Lord your God has commanded you.
—Deuteronomy 5:33 (NIV)

What do you think about when you read that scripture? Maybe the Ten Commandments, or maybe pleasing God by doing what He says in His Word.

I remember a time in my teenage years when I thought I had the worst parents in the world. They had rules for me to live by, and I didn't like a lot of them. Why can't I spend time with my friends if my chores aren't finished? Why do I have to clean my room every week? Why do I have to be home from a date at 11 p.m. when most of my friends get to stay out later? My attitude toward my dad was not always very good because of all the *rules!* In Colossians 3:20 (NKJV), the Bible says, "Children, obey your parents in all things, for this is well pleasing to the Lord."

After I became an adult and was out in the world on my own, I began to understand why my dad and mom had given me boundaries. They taught me respect, responsibility, and that there are consequences for my actions and decisions. They taught me right from wrong and tried to teach me how to live life and be a good person.

That is what God teaches us in His Word. He is our "heavenly Father," and He wants us to be obedient to Him because He knows what we need better than we know ourselves. Matthew 6:32 (NKJV) says, "For Your heavenly Father knows that you need all these things." What things? Food, clothing, and basic needs. (Please read Matthew 6:25–32 NKJV.) If we seek Him first, He gives us a promise. In Matthew 6:33 (NKJV), Jesus says, "But seek first the Kingdom of God and His righteousness, and all these things shall be added to you." Jesus doesn't say *may* be, but *shall* be. That means He *definitely* will!

So I ask you today, will you be obedient to God? Will you seek Him *first*? If you do, and you are obedient, you *will* be blessed.

Father, please help us to be obedient to You just because You are our heavenly Father, because we love You, and because it is the right thing to do. Amen.

# 62

## Church

And I also say to you that you are Peter, and on this rock I will build my church, and the gates of Hades shall not prevail against it.

—Matthew 16:18 (NKJV)

What do you think of when your hear the word *church?* Do you think of a building, a place to worship, or do you think of the body of believers?

In Matthew 16:13–20 (NKJV), the Bible talks about Peter's confession of Jesus as the Christ. The word *petra* is Greek for "rock," and the word *petros* is Greek for "Peter." In verse 18, Jesus was saying that it was the truth that Peter confessed, that Jesus *was* the Christ, and on this He would build His church.

Today, there are many denominations, and in each one there are different traditions and usually some differing beliefs. It is important we look for *truth* when searching for a church home, a body of believers to worship with and become a part of their church family. Is the pastor preaching and teaching the Word of God? Does it align with the scriptures in the Bible? Truth is truth, even when sometimes we really don't want to hear it. I love what a pastor said once: "You don't know what you don't know until you know it! Then you can never unknow it!" (I take a lot of notes in church.) Sometimes the truth and what God wants us to learn is difficult, but it's always necessary if we are to continue to grow to become more like Christ. Life is not about what we want but about what God wants to do through us.

In Colossians 1:24 (TPT), Paul says, "I can even celebrate the sorrows I have experienced on your behalf; for as I join with you in your difficulties, it helps you to discover what lacks *in your understanding* of the sufferings Jesus Christ experienced for his body, the church." Paul was saying Christians will suffer in this world because Christ suffered, but Paul counted it as joy because it would be rewarded in eternity. Christ said in John 16:33 (TPT):

> And everything I have taught you is so that the peace which is in me will be in you and will give you great confidence as you rest in me. For in this unbelieving world you will experience trouble and sorrows, but you must be courageous, for I have conquered the world!

Jesus died for us all! Will you live for Him and be part of His church, regardless of the cost?

Thank You Father, that You sent Jesus to die for us so that we can live with You in heaven for eternity. Thank You that we can be part of a church family and proclaim Your gospel! Amen.

# 63

## Priorities

But seek first the kingdom of God and His righteousness, and all these things shall be added to you.

—Matthew 6:33 (NKJV)

Priorities. What do you think of when you hear the word *priorities?* Do you think of your to-do list and what needs to be finished first? Do you think of your job, bills, and family? What do you think Jesus would think about the word *priorities?*

According to the previous scripture, which is spoken by Jesus, we are to "seek first the kingdom of God and His righteousness" (Matthew 6:33 NKJV). This simply means we are to concentrate on seeking God's will for our lives, putting Him first—He should be our priority. We are not to worry; we are to trust Him. When putting God first, we need to leave all other matters to Him, trusting Him to handle them. Jesus then states, "All these things will be added to you" (Matthew 6:33 NKJV). What "things"? Please read Matthew 6:25–32. Jesus is telling us that if we put God first, make *Him* our priority, and trust and don't worry, then our needs will be met. Simple, right?

Well, it might be simple, but it is not necessarily easy. In Matthew 6:34 (NKJV), Jesus tells us, "Therefore do not worry about tomorrow, for tomorrow will worry about its own things. Sufficient for the day is its own trouble." We are to live one day at a time. There will be problems, but we are to face them with faith and trust God to see us through each day.

Will you make God your priority today?

Father, please help us start each day with You, to make You our priority, then trust You to meet our needs. Thank You for loving us so much! Amen.

# 64

## Testimony

I find words to be very interesting and the way people interpret them even more interesting. I have heard it said that without a test, there would be no testimony. In the previous scripture, Jesus is telling us that we *will* have tribulation, so—what do we do with it? Do we use it to make us bitter or better?

We find the word *testimony* used in the Bible in Exodus 16:34 (NKJV): "As the Lord commanded Moses, so Aaron laid it up before the Testimony, to be kept." Here, the word testimony was referring to the tablets of law, also known as the Ten Commandments. I found this very interesting. The human race needed laws to follow to be the kind of people God wanted them to be. When tribulations, or tests, came about, they could look at what God had given them to help them make the right choices.

Do we do that now? When we are faced with tribulation, tests, and trials in life, do we look to God for our answers? If we do and we make the right choices, then God is glorified and pleased.

Sometimes when we think of the word testimony, we might also think of the word *witness*. Will you be a good witness for our loving Father God?

Father, please help us look to You for the choices and decisions we must make in life so that, with our testimony, we may glorify You with all that we say and do and be a good witness for You. Amen.

# 65

## Extravagant Love

Love never fails.

—1 Corinthians 13:8 (NKJV)

Love is the absolute greatest gift ever, but has there been a time in your life when you did not feel loved? There are many reasons why we might feel unloved. Maybe you have been through a difficult family situation, or have been through a divorce, or are a single person living alone.

First John 4:8 (NKJV) says, "He who does not love does not know God, for God is love." God did not just create love; He *is* love! One thing you can be sure of is God's love for us. He sent Jesus to be born in a stable with smelly animals, and His bed was straw in a manger where typically animals would eat their food—not the best of conditions for a king to be born! Jesus's sole purpose for coming to earth as a human was because of love. John 3:16 (NKJV) says, "For God so loved the world that He gave His only begotten Son, that whoever believes in Him should not perish but have everlasting life." That is not just love—that is extravagant love! Is there anyone in your life willing to die for you? If you would have been the only person on the earth, Jesus would still have died for you!

First Corinthians 13 is known as the "Love Chapter." Please read it. (The Passion Translation is really good, but pick your favorite version.)

Human affection can fail. We need to learn to love others with the same kind of unselfish love that God pours out on us continually—extravagant love. God's love for us will never end!

Is there someone you can show the love of Jesus to today?

Father God, thank You for Your extravagant love. Help us to love others the way You love us. Amen.

# 66

# Discernment

> For the Word of God is living and powerful, and sharper than any two-edged sword, piercing even to the division of soul and spirit, and joints and marrow, and is a discerner of the thoughts and intents of the heart.
>
> —Hebrews 4:12 (NKJV)

Opinions—we all have them, so how do we decide what our opinions are? What is the *basis* for our opinions? As Christ followers, we are to glorify God with all we say and do. That would include our spoken opinions. I am pretty sure we should not base our opinions on the opinions of others. The Bible tells us God has given us a sound mind. In 2 Timothy 1:7 (NKJV), it says, "For God has not given us a spirit of fear, but of power and of love and of a sound mind."

Is it right for us to form an opinion of, say, a book or a movie because of someone else's opinion or review? We know the basic content from reading the short description on the inside cover of a book or seeing the trailer of a movie, at least most of the time. Undoubtedly, as Christ followers, there are books and movies we should *not* read or see because of the obvious questionable content. Some things are pretty obvious, however others are not. So should we allow people to influence our decisions?

Maybe we should do our own research, check what the Bible says, and then discern what God is saying to us through the Holy Spirit. Listen to what Jesus says in Matthew 16:2–3 (NKJV):

> He answered and said to them, "When it is evening you say, 'It will be fair weather for the sky is red'; and in the morning, 'It will be foul weather today for the sky is red and threatening!' Hypocrites! You know how to discern the face of the sky, but you cannot discern the signs of the times!"

The world wants to influence us and our opinions, but so does God: "Greater is He that is in me than He that is in the world" (1 John 4:4 KJV).

Who will you let influence your decisions?

Father God, thank You for sending the Holy Spirit to be our helper so that we can glorify You with the decisions we make. Amen.

# 67

## Family

For God so loved the world.

—John 3:16 (NKJV)

Family is special. God gave us all a family for a reason, or maybe even many reasons. The nucleus of the family is the father and mother, then come the children, in most families. We are family forever. Families have their happy times and sad times, blessed times and difficult times, but no matter what—we are always family.

My brother lives several hours away, and we don't get to spend as much time together as I wish we could, so the time we do spend together is always special. No matter what, he will *always* be my brother.

God wants each and every one of us to be part of His family. He created the world, then Adam and Eve for His companions. (Please read Genesis chapter 1 NKJV.) The earth was a perfect place, then the fall of man happened. Sin came into the world and changed everything.

We have a loving, heavenly Father who sent His only son into the world to redeem the world. First John 4:14 (KJV) says, "And we have seen and do testify that the Father sent the Son to be the Savior of the World." God loves each one of us and wants us *all* to be part of

His family. Most of us are familiar with John 3:16 (NKJV): "For God so loved the world that He gave His only begotten Son, that whoever believes in Him should not perish but have everlasting life."

Sometimes things happen in human families that make family members choose to *not* be part of that family any longer, even though God's plan is for family to always be family. It is the same with us as God's children; some choose to *not* be part of God's family, but that is never His plan. The Bible says in 2 Peter 3:9 (NKJV), "The Lord is not slack concerning His promise, as some count slackness, but is long-suffering toward us, not willing that any should perish but that all would come to repentance." So then, you might ask, "What promise?" Peter is reminding us of the promise that someday Jesus *will* return. When He does, it will be to take His family to heaven for eternity—*if* we have chosen to be part of it.

Will you choose to be part of God's family?

Father God, thank You for family—our earthly families, but most of all our heavenly family. Amen.

# 68

# The Lighthouse

God is our refuge and strength, a very present help in trouble.

—Psalm 46:1 (NKJV)

What do you think of when you think about a lighthouse? I think of several things: a beautiful structure by the sea, the beam of light that glows from it at night, and how it is a picture of safety in the storms that sometimes rage in the oceans. Then I think of Jesus and how He is our safety and light—*always*. When days are sunny and clear and when the storms of life rage, He is there. He tells us He will never leave us or forsake us. (Please read Hebrews 13:5 NKJV.)

I have a picture in my mind I have tried to draw, but I am not an artist. Try as I might, I cannot put it on paper. It is a picture of a coast with a tall bluff, and at its base, at sea level, there are some large boulders and other smaller rocks. On top of that bluff stands a lighthouse, tall, majestic, and strong. Below, further from the rocks, is a sandy beach with some sea oats growing in several places while the sea is rushing to the shore and seagulls are flying above. The sky is blue, and the sun is shining. It is such a vivid picture in my mind that I can almost hear the seagulls and the sound of the surf and feel the sea spray on my face! It is a very happy place for me. I love the ocean because, for whatever reasons, I feel at peace there. But in an instant, it can become a raging sea! Just like life—one minute calm and the next a storm! But there is good news! Jesus is our lighthouse! He will guide us to safety and peace in every storm of life.

There is a story in Mark 4:35–41 (NKJV) where Jesus and His disciples are in a boat on the Sea of Galilee, and a storm comes up. Jesus is sleeping but is awakened by frightened disciples. He speaks to the wind and sea, and they become calm. He will calm our storms in life if we ask, believe, and trust Him.

Thank You, Lord, for being that beacon of light that will always bring us back to You and safety in the rough waters of life. Amen.

*Marshall Point Light in Maine*

# 69

## Freedom

Therefore, if the Son makes you free, you shall be free indeed.

—John 8:36 (NKJV)

Every Fourth of July, we celebrate freedom and remember all those who in the service of our country in the military sacrificed their lives to give us that freedom. There is another freedom we need to celebrate. In the previous verse, it says that "the Son makes us free" (John 8:36 NKJV). Jesus died on that cross for us *all* so we can be free from sin and death and live with Him in heaven for eternity. Those are Jesus's words! I recently heard a fairly new Christ follower say, "Read the red words in the Bible; they are the most important words!" He is right! Those are the words spoken by Jesus.

Sometimes those who have been Christ followers for a long time can become complacent and maybe even ungrateful. I believe God uses new believers who are on fire for God—so thankful for the forgiveness and the joy that they experience—to remind those who have been His followers for a while of what the Bible says in Romans 8:2 (NKJV): "The law of the Spirit of life in Christ Jesus has made us free from the law of sin and death."

If you think, for whatever reason, your freedom has become boring, or if you are tending to focus more on the negative and things you

135

can't do, then think about this: Romans 6:22 (NIV) says, "But now that you have been set free from sin and have become slaves of God, the benefit you reap leads to holiness, and the result is eternal life." That is a freedom we should celebrate daily! To be a slave means to be controlled by someone. Do you want to be controlled by God to eternal life in heaven or to be controlled by sin to eternal damnation and hell?

Father, thank You for the United States of America and the freedom to live and worship as we choose. Thank You for the freedom we experience as followers of Jesus Christ, and help us to share that freedom with others. Amen.

# 70

# My Son Room

Cause me to hear Your lovingkindness in the morning, for in You do I trust; cause me to know the way in which I should walk, for I lift up my soul to You.

—Psalm 143:8 (NKJV)

I enjoy and look forward to spending time with God every morning. That is also when I typically write, but not always. It seems that is when I am inspired—maybe because I am already focused on God. I sit in my sunroom, which I now enjoy calling my "Son Room" (thanks to a friend's suggestion), having coffee in the mornings. It is quiet, I am rested after a good night's sleep, and I have a beautiful view. I truly treasure my mornings with God, especially when I write.

When Jesus was on earth, He also would spend time with His Father early in the morning. One account is in Mark 1:35 (NKJV): "Now in the morning, having risen a long while before daylight, He went out and departed to a solitary place; and there He prayed." This scripture indicates that Christ needed solitude. He needed a time to be with His Father to gain perspective and to renew His energy. His ministry was preaching and teaching, casting out demons, and healing the sick. He could not risk exhausting His energy and losing His perspective, so He was always communing with His Father.

He was one-hundred percent God, but He was also one-hundred percent human.

I find when I put God first by reading His Word and praying, seeking His will and direction for my day, that it makes my day much better. We should be attentive to God all through our day, not just during our quiet time or devotion time. When we are in tune with the Holy Spirit within us, He will direct our day much better than we can.

Will you start your day with God and let Him give you direction?

Father, thank You for life. Help me through Your Holy Spirit within me to make You part of my day, every day. Amen.

# 71

# The Fence

When having a conversation of a spiritual nature and decisions are being debated, I often say, "If you have not chosen Christ, you have made a choice." In Matthew 12:30 (TPT), Jesus says, "So join me, for if you're not on my side you are against me. And if you refuse to help me gather the spoils, you are making things worse."

I recently returned from a mission trip to Kentucky, and in a conversation our team had one morning during devotions, I made the statement, "If you have not chosen Christ, you have made a choice." The next day, a young man Evan Jennerjahn, who was in high school at the time and was on our team, did the morning devotions. He said that when I said "If you have not chosen Christ, you have made a choice," it reminded him of a story he had heard from one of the leaders while on a youth trip with church. He shared it with us, so I am going to share it with you (in my words, and not nearly as good as he told it):

There was a man who was sitting on a fence. On one side was God. God invited him to come over to His side and told him he could have good things: love, salvation, forgiveness, and eternity in heaven with Him. The man was unsure, so he said, "Not now, but I'll think about it." On the other side of the fence was Satan. Satan invited him to come join him, and he promised have fun: drinking, sex, drugs, and lots of partying. The man didn't really want that, so he told Satan, "No, not now." He just continued to stay on the fence. Soon the day came when the man died. Satan came to get him, but the man exclaimed, "I didn't come over to your side!" Satan owned the fence!

So you see, if we don't choose Christ, we have made a choice. If you haven't made a choice, do you want to take a chance that Satan owns the fence you are on? Satan is the master of lies, and the only power he has is what we give him. However, God always has power, and He wants us on His side of the fence.

In the familiar scripture John 3:16 (NKJV), it says, "For God so loved the world that He gave His only begotten Son, that whoever believes in Him should not perish but have everlasting life."

Will you get off the fence and choose Jesus today?

Thank You, Father, for sending Jesus to die on the cross so that we can repent, have our sins forgiven, and live with You forever in Heaven. Help us to make the right choice. Amen.

# 72

## Rewards

Do you like receiving rewards? Most of us do. When we are teaching our children to listen to our instructions, be obedient, and be responsible, we often use some sort of reward system. It helps motivate them and teach them to make good choices and decisions.

Jesus does the same thing with us. In Mark 10:29 (NIV), Jesus is asking that He be made the priority, and in Mark 10:30, if that happens, there will be spiritual rewards for those who choose to follow. Those spiritual rewards are priceless. Jesus also says there will be persecutions, but in Matthew 5:10 (NIV), He gives us a promise: "Blessed are those who are persecuted for righteousness sake, for theirs is the kingdom of Heaven." This is the ultimate reward!

In Mark 10:17–21(NIV) is the story of the rich young ruler who asked Jesus how to have eternal life. Jesus told him to go and sell his possessions and give the money to the poor, then come and follow Him, but the young ruler was not willing to do that. So what did he miss out on because of his choice? He trusted in His riches instead of Christ.

In John 10:9–10 (NIV), Jesus says, "I am the gate; whoever enters through me will be saved. They will come in and out, and find pasture. The thief comes only to steal and kill and destroy; I have come that they may have life, and have it to the full." Jesus wants us not only to have eternal life, but abundant life on earth—His reward to us for putting Him first while we are on earth, *then* eternal life with Him! There is no better reward.

Father, please help us to follow Jesus and make Him the priority of our lives so that we can live a satisfying life on earth and then be with Him for eternity. Amen.

# 73

## The Tithe

"Bring the whole tithe into the storehouse, that there may be food in my house. Test me in this," says the Lord Almighty, "and see if I will not throw open the floodgates of heaven and pour out so much blessing that there will not be room enough to store it."

—Malachi 3:10 (NIV)

What do you think of when you hear the word *tithe?* I have only heard it used in conversations concerning scripture. The word tithe means "to give one tenth." There are many places in the Bible, in the Old and New Testaments, that it talks about tithes. It is a subject that is not really popular because it involves giving what we think is ours, but is it really ours? I think not. This earth and everything in it and all that we have belong to God. So why does God want us to tithe? I believe (and I am by no stretch of the imagination a Bible scholar—not even close!) because of going to church, reading and studying the Bible, and being in Bible study groups, that there are several reasons. God does not need our 10 percent, we should *want* to be good stewards of what God has given us. We should *want* to give because we love God and *want* to be obedient to Him. We should *want* to give to help others.

There are reasons why God wants us to be obedient, but we don't always understand. The Bible is God's inspired Word, or

God-breathed Word. (Please read 2 Timothy 3:16–17 NIV.) Two of the main things we are to do as Christ followers is trust God and obey His Word. Can you imagine what a different world it would be if *every* Christ follower would give 10 percent of their income?

What is God asking you to give?

Father, thank You for all that You so graciously give us. Help us to always look to You for guidance and direction in our lives and for answers to all our questions, then help us to be obedient to You. Amen.

# 74

# Who Am I In Christ.

Have you ever thought about who you are in Christ? There are many scriptures that tell us. One is the previous scripture, which is one of my favorites. It says when we accept Christ as our personal savior, we become a new person. Our sins are forgiven, so we start life again with our focus on Jesus, doing what is right and good and staying in His will for our lives. The words of Paul in 2 Corinthians 5:17 (NKJV) are words of hope. I am a new creation!

I am blessed. Psalm 32:1 (NKJV) says, "Blessed is he whose transgression is forgiven, whose sin is covered." We have joy because of forgiveness.

I am dead to sin. In Romans 6:11 (NKJV) it says, "Likewise, you also, reckon yourselves to be dead indeed to sin, but alive to God in Christ Jesus our Lord." In this scripture, Paul is giving us the beginning of a plan of action for our new life.

God values each one of us because we are all His children. He sent His only son to die for us! Salvation is a gift to be received by each person. It is sad that some choose not to accept that gift. Jesus loves us all, and we are all precious to Him. It is not God's will that even one should perish! Please read Matthew 18:10–14 (NKJV).

Who are you in Christ today?

Father, thank You that I am Yours and that You love me. Amen.

# 75

# Storms

---

You, Lord, are my lamp; the Lord turns my darkness into light.

—2 Samuel 22:29 (NIV)

---

Recently, there were bad storms where I live and all throughout northern and central Indiana. Those storms produced at least six tornados. Power was lost in a very large area, including where I live. It was early afternoon when I lost power, so I thought the it would come back on soon. Night came, and still no power. Life is very different when we do not have the things we are used to having to make life comfortable. A friend had come to visit, so I lit oil lamps and we sat at the kitchen table and played games, talked, and enjoyed each other's company, laughing about the "adventure" we were on together.

In a Bible study I was in, we were studying Acts, and I thought about Paul and Silas being put in prison and how they handled that situation. In Acts 16:25 (NKJV), it says, "But at midnight, Paul and Silas were praying and singing hymns to God, and the prisoners were listening to them."

I guess what we need to learn is that no matter what happens in life, it is how we respond that matters. We need to grow with the challenges that life gives us. We need to always find hope in every situation. What do you think the prisoners thought when they heard Paul and Silas singing praises to God at midnight? They were trusting God to see them through. (Please take time to read Acts 16:25–34 NKJV.) Their reaction to a very difficult situation had a profound impact on many.

How do you handle the storms of life? Is Jesus your light in darkness?

Thank You Lord that You walk with us through the storms of life and that You will always be our light in the darkness. Amen.

*Storm coming over the mountains in Montego Bay, Jamaica*

# 76

## Seeing

Then the righteous will answer Him, saying, "Lord, when did we see You hungry and feed You, or thirsty and give You drink? When did we see You a stranger and take You in, or naked and clothe You? Or when did we see You sick, or in prison and come to You?"
—Matthew 25:37–39 (NKJV)

Some of us wear glasses. I wore glasses most of my life until I had cataract surgery several years ago. I only need to wear them now to read. There are lots of requirements for those wearing glasses, and they are all different for each person. We each need the right prescription. We need to see, and with the proper glasses we have a new perspective on life.

It is the same with Jesus. When He is not in our lives, we see things differently. When we have Him in our lives, He gives us a much clearer perspective on life. We see how blessed we are and also how many needs there are around us. We need to see people through the eyes of Jesus.

So what can we do with our new vision? We need to live different lives, ones of caring, helping, and compassion. Matthew 25:40 (NKJV) says, "And the King will answer and say to them, 'Assuredly,

I say to you, inasmuch as you did *it* to one of the least of these My brethren, you did *it* to me.'"

It is the quality of the lens that makes all the difference. How have we helped "the least of these" in what we have done today or this week (Matthew 25:40 NKJV)? Did we "feed His sheep?" (Please read John 21:17 NKJV.)

Lord, please help us see You in the lost, the hungry, and the broken. May we love them, help them, and tell them about You. Amen.

# 77

## Faith

So what exactly is this faith we hear talked about? Some words used to define it are: trust, expectation, and hope.

Chapter 11 of Hebrews (NKJV) is known as the faith chapter. In the forty verses of this chapter, the word faith is used twenty-four times, not counting subtitles. There are many examples in that short chapter of a life of faith, and there are many heroes of faith listed.

If God gives us so many examples of faith lived out in this many lives, I would say He really, really wants us to understand faith. We should be convinced in the reality of God after reading all the examples in this chapter. Please take time to read the whole chapter and meditate on what God is telling us. There is a good reason why God wants us to understand faith. Look at Hebrews 11:6 (NKJV): "But without faith it is impossible to please Him, for he who comes to God must believe that He is and that He is a rewarder of those who diligently seek Him."

Think about it this way: living by faith is acting like God is telling the truth, and having no faith means calling God a liar, challenging

God's integrity. So the question is: will you believe God today and walk by faith or call Him a liar?

Father, thank You for Your Word and giving us the Bible so we can learn and understand and then live a life that pleases You. Amen.

# 78

## Are You Teachable.

Are you teachable? Some people are, but some may not be. Are you willing to accept new truth from God? Sometimes we get stuck in a rut or we get comfortable where we are. Change is sometimes, probably even most of the time, uncomfortable. Maybe it is easier to stay where we are than to step out in faith because of something God is teaching or trying to teach us. Sometimes Satan will come in and try to discourage us, confuse us, or even make us fearful to keep us from what God has for us, but God gives us many promises and much encouragement in His Word:

- "Little children, *you can be certain that* you belong to God and have conquered them, for the One who is living in you is far greater than the one who is in the world." (1 John 4:4 TPT)
- "For God has not given us the spirit of fear; but of power, and of love and of a sound mind." (2 Timothy 1:7 NKJV)
- "Delight yourself also in the Lord and He shall give you the desires of your heart. Commit your way to the Lord, trust also in Him, and He shall bring it to pass." (Psalm 37:4–5 NKJV)

These passages mean consciously commit all your plans to the Lord, daily. Do not presume His help if it is uninvited.

Sometimes people blame Satan, when in reality it is a lack of obedience to God or a bad decision or choice that causes us to face troubling circumstances. Some people might say Satan can influence us without us knowing, and I agree, *but* God has given us everything we need to fight those *fiery darts* from the evil one! (Please read Ephesians 6:16 NKJV.) That is why it is so important to be in God's Word daily and spend time in prayer with our Father.

Are you willing to allow God to teach you today?

Father, forgive us for not listening, not trusting, and not being obedient. Please help us today to hear, trust, and obey only You. Amen.

# 79

# Humble and Kind

He has shown you, O man, what is good; and what does the Lord require of you but to do justly, to love mercy, and to walk humbly with your God?

—Micah 6:8 (NKJV)

What exactly does humble mean? It simply means not proud or arrogant, and my favorite definition: courteously respectful. Another word that goes hand in hand with humble is *kind*. Kind, simply put, means to be indulgent, gentle, and considerate.

One time in a conversation with my cousin, she said it is better to be kind than right. That, to me, was a pretty profound statement filled with wisdom, and I have never forgotten it. How many times in life do we, in whatever way, try to always be right?

According to the above verse in Micah, being humble is a requirement, and if it is a requirement, it is extremely important to God. Some opposites to being humble could be showy, conceited, or egotistical, which simply means *self*-centered, *self*-involved, or *self*-seeking. There are more words to explain it, but that is enough to make my point, which is: do you see the common denominator there? (A hint: self.)

We all have things we need to work on. In Romans 3:10 (NKJV), the Bible says, "As it is written, there is none righteous, no, not one."

God loves us so much He shows us mercy, every day! Lamentations 3:22–23 (NKJV) says, "Through the Lord's mercies we are not consumed, because His compassions fail not. They are new every morning; Great is Your Faithfulness." I am so very grateful His mercies are new every day and that He has such compassion for us—the reason is because He loves us so much! We should strive to be humble because God wants us to be humble.

I recently lost a longtime, dear, dear, friend. She went home to be with Jesus. She was the most kind and humble woman I have ever known. She never had a negative or harsh word to say about anyone, and she put everyone's needs before her own, always! That is the way God wants us each to live. We don't need to be showy, conceited, or self-centered to feel important or to get the attention we think we need or deserve. James 4:10 (NKJV) says, "Humble yourselves in the sight of the Lord, and He will lift you up."

Lord, please help us to be humble and kind to each other, today and always. Amen.

# 80

## Harsh Words

Have you ever spoken badly to someone or had someone say very hurtful things to you? I think most of us would say "yes" on both accounts. We are human, and God gave us our emotions. However, we should learn how to control them and not let our emotions control us.

If our emotions do get out of control, it is important we acknowledge it, see the hurt it caused, repent, and ask not only God to forgive us, but also the person who we hurt with our words. We are always supposed to forgive. In Matthew 18:21–22, Peter asked Jesus this: "Then Peter came to Him and said, 'Lord, how often shall my brother sin against me, and I forgive him? Up to seven times?' Jesus said to him, 'I do not say to you, up to seven times but seventy times seven'" (NKJV). In other words, we are to always forgive. I do not believe we are to forget the incident because we don't want to fall into that situation again, but we are to forget the pain it caused. In Proverbs 15:1–2 (NKJV), it says, "A soft answer turns away wrath, but a harsh word stirs up anger. The tongue of the wise uses knowledge rightly, but the mouth of fools pours forth foolishness."

I believe if people continue to hurt us with their words after trying to address the issues, then we have decisions to make as to whether or not that is a healthy relationship. Once in a Sunday school class I was in, we did a study about taking care of our souls. I had not really given much thought to my soul until that study. We know we have to keep our bodies and minds healthy, but what about our souls? First Timothy 6:6 (NKJV) says, "Now godliness with contentment is great gain." I believe that if we are content, we are at peace, and if we are at peace, that is good for our soul. A question we might ask is, "Is it healing to be around me?" That question deserves some serious thought.

God has shown me since I started writing how important the words are that we speak. The harsh words leave scars and separate people. We should strive to say positive words—words that encourage, comfort, and show love. With God's help we can do that. Sometimes things come up that are controversial or negative or there are differing opinions, and those things need to be handled with love in the correct manner.

How will you use your words today?

Father, we are all human, make mistakes, and say things we shouldn't. Help our words to be positive, healing, and to bring Glory to You! Amen.

# 81

# Superheroes

> But those who wait on the Lord shall renew their strength; they shall mount up with wings like eagles, they shall run and not be weary, they shall walk and not faint.
>
> —Isaiah 40:31 (NKJV)

If you have children or grandchildren, you probably know about superheroes who always save the day at just the right moment. When I was young, it was Superman, then there was Batman, Spiderman, Wonder Woman, and the list goes on. They all seem to be very busy, and their work is very difficult, but they always prevail.

There are many superheroes in the Bible as well (read Hebrews chapter 11 NKJV): Noah, who *by faith* built an Ark; Abraham, who *by faith* was ready to sacrifice his son Isaac; Moses, who *by faith* parted the Red Sea; and these are only a few of many.

We really don't know where those cartoon characters got their superpowers, but we know that the Bible heroes got all of their power *by faith* from God who is the master of the universe! In Isaiah 43:2–3, it says:

> When you pass through the waters, I will be with you; and through the rivers, they shall not overflow

you. When you walk through the fire, you shall not be burned, nor shall the flame scorch you. For I am the Lord your God, the Holy One of Israel, your Savior. (NKJV)

In Isaiah 46:4 the Bible says, "Even to your old age, I am He. And even to gray hairs I will carry you! I have made, and I will bear; even I will carry and deliver you."(NKJV)

The superhero for all who are Christ followers is three in one: God the Father, Christ the Son, and the Holy Spirit who dwells within each of us. So—we are never alone!
Hebrews 13:8 (NKJV) says, "Jesus Christ is the same yesterday, today and forever." What an *awesome* superhero!

Thank You Lord for always being there for us, even when we don't think You are, and please forgive our unbelief. Amen.

# 82

# Are You Hungry.

For He satisfies the longing soul, and fills the hungry with goodness.

—Psalm 107:9 (NKJV)

Are you sometimes hungry for something but can't figure out what it is you are hungry for? Maybe it isn't food for your body that is needed, but food for your soul.

Psalm 107 (NKJV) is a psalm of thanksgiving. The psalmist is talking about how God meets the needs of the people, and how He delivers them. The psalmist starts in Psalm 107:1 (NKJV) by saying, "Oh give thanks to the Lord, for He is good! For His mercy endures forever." Four times the psalmist says in Psalm 107 (NKJV), "Oh, that men would give thanks to the Lord for His goodness." (See verses 8a, 15a, 21a, and 31a, and please take time to read all of Psalm 107.)

This psalm was part of my Bible reading today, and it really began to speak to me about living a life of thanksgiving no matter what we are going through in our lives. The people of Israel were wandering in the wilderness in the desert of Sinai, and God took care of them! He met all of their needs! Their clothes and shoes did not wear out, they had shelter, and God provided food and water for them every day.

"He delivered them out of their distresses," we are told four times in these forty-three verses of Psalm 107 (6, 13b, 19b, 28b NKJV). This psalm truly shows God's loving kindness, salvation, and provision. What can be more loving than a God who continually meets our needs? There is not one person on the earth who is as loving and caring and who can do for us what God does *if* we love Him, trust Him, and obey Him. This psalm is full of great wisdom, and it reminds us over and over of God's deliverance, love, and provision, and that we need to praise Him for His great love.

The psalm ends with this verse: "Whoever is wise will observe these things, and they will understand the loving kindness of the Lord" (Psalm 107:43 NKJV).

Are you hungry for God's Word?

Father, please help us to praise You for the Great love that You show us, give us a hunger for Your Word, and help us live a life of thanksgiving. Amen.

# 83

## Say Yes, Lord

I recently returned from a mission trip to Jamaica. There was a team made up of American ladies and Jamaican ladies that lead a three-day Christian retreat with twenty other Jamaican ladies as guests. The purpose of the retreat was to shut out the distractions of the world and totally focus on God so we could better hear His voice and most importantly feel loved—not only by God, but by each other.

Our theme song for the three days was "Yes, Lord, Yes" written by Shirley Caesar, and it is one of those songs that stays with you for a long time when you hear it! You should look it up and listen to it. It talks about saying yes to God, trusting and obeying Him no matter what.

In our everyday lives, sometimes the busyness of work, family, and other obligations keeps us from spending quality time with God. Because of that, we could miss something profound or important that God wants to say to us, so we need to regularly set aside time to be in God's presence.

At this retreat, lives were changed, there was healing and restoration for some, and a faith was renewed for others. Psalm 139:23–24 (NKJV) says, "Search me, O God, and know my heart; try me, and know my anxieties; and see if there is any wicked way in me, and lead me in the way everlasting."

As Christ followers, we want to grow, learn, and hear God's voice, but Satan wants none of that. He is happy when we are distracted and too busy. You don't have to go on a retreat, but you can set aside time to say, "Yes, Lord, I want to hear from You!"

Will you do that today?

Father, in these busy lives we live, help us to make time for You! Help us to find time to read Your Word, pray, and hear Your plans for our lives. Amen.

# 84

# Wise or Foolish.

The fear of the Lord is the beginning of knowledge,
but fools despise wisdom and instruction.
—Proverbs 1:7 (NKJV)

I have been reading a chapter in Proverbs every day because I learn something every time I do. It is full of wisdom. God says in Proverbs 3:13–14 (NKJV), "Happy *is* the man *who* finds wisdom, and the man *who* gains understanding; for her proceeds are better than the profits of silver, and her gain than fine gold." Who wouldn't want that? We are to try to live a good life, pleasing to God, not men.

Solomon wrote most of the Proverbs, and it is said that his passion was for knowledge and wisdom, which is certainly reflected in the book of Proverbs. It is a book of practical ethics that emphasizes righteousness and the fear of God.

The fear of God basically means having knowledge of God and being submissive to His will—not being afraid of God. He is our loving Father who wants the best for us and has given us instructions in His Word how to do that. When the word *fools* is used, it is referring to those who have rejected wisdom, therefore rejecting God. This is what is being talked about in Proverbs 1:7 (NKJV). It also uses the word *despise*, so those are some pretty strong words directed toward "fools."

In Proverbs 1:5 it says, "A wise man will hear and increase learning, and a man of understanding will attain wise counsel," and Proverbs 1:33 says, "But whoever listens to me will dwell safely, and will be secure, without fear of evil" (NKJV). Proverbs 14:9 states, "Fools mock at sin, but among the upright *there is* favor."

So my question to you today is this: do you want to be wise or foolish?

Father, thank You for Your Word, which gives us knowledge. Help us to seek it along with understanding and wisdom so we can live a victorious life. Amen.

# 85

## Live, Love, Laugh

And so we know and rely on the love God has for
us. God is love. Whoever lives in love lives in God,
and God in them.

—1 John 4:16 (NIV)

"Live, Love, Laugh." This is one of those popular sayings that has
been around for quite a long time, so I decided to see what the Bible
had to say about those three words.

I really like the part of 1 John 4:16 that says, "God is love" (NIV).
That is a very profound statement. God is not just the creator of love;
He *is* love! Think about that!
Jude 1:21 (NKJV) says, "Keep yourselves in the love of God, looking
for the mercy of our Lord Jesus Christ unto eternal life." In other
words, we need to maintain our lives with God. Jude is encouraging
us to stay in that love so we cannot be separated from it. (Please read
Romans 8:35–39 NKJV.)

Romans 8:13 (NKJV) says, "For if you live according to the flesh,
you will die; but if by the Spirit you put to death the deeds of the
body, you will live." Romans 12:16 (NIV) states, "Live in harmony
with one another. Do not be proud but be willing to associate with
people of low position. Do not be conceited."

If we would live like this and love and help each other, it would be a different world. Some people think too highly of themselves. God loves us all, and in Romans 12:3 it says this, "For by the grace given me I say to every one of you: Do not think of yourself more highly than you ought, but rather think of yourself with sober judgement, in accordance with the faith God has distributed to each of you" (NIV).

I believe God wants us to enjoy the life He has given us, but He also wants us to walk with Him every minute of every day.

The last word of the three is laugh. Psalm 126:2–3 (NIV) says, "Our mouths were filled with laughter, our tongues with songs of joy. Then it was said among the nations, 'The Lord has done great things for us, and we are filled with joy.'"

Will you allow God to help you daily to live, love, and laugh?

Father God, we thank You for the life You have given each of us and ask that You help us to live it the way You want us to. Help us love each other and laugh often. Amen.

# 86

# Fishing

Then He said to them, "Follow Me, and I will make you fishers of men."
—Matthew 4:19 (NKJV)

When I was a very young girl growing up, my dad and grandpa loved to go fishing, so I developed a love for it as well. My grandpa bought me a pair of jeans and a shirt and cut off one of his belts to fit me, and that was my "fishing outfit." He would make dough balls for bait and take me to the Mississinewa River, and we would catch sunfish. At the time, I didn't realize the memories we were making. As an adult, one summer my goal was to out-fish my dad. We spent many hours on the lake that summer, just me and my dad. I cherish these memories of fishing.

When Jesus began His ministry, he left Nazareth to live in the city of Capernaum in the area of Galilee, by the Sea of Galilee. Matthew 4:18 (NKJV) says, "And Jesus, walking by the Sea of Galilee saw two brothers, Simon called Peter, and Andrew his brother, casting a net into the sea for they were fishermen." Then something pretty amazing and profound happened! Matthew 4:19–20 (NKJV) says, "Then He said to them, 'Follow Me and I will make you fishers of men.' They immediately left their nets and followed Him." This was their job, how they earned a living, and they willingly walked away from probably the family business that they grew up being part of.

To do what? To become "fishers of men." I wonder if they had any idea what that even meant.

Jesus had a plan, like He always does. He called, Peter and Andrew answered the call, they were obedient, and the rest is history—they became disciples. But when they left with Jesus, it was just the beginning! The beginning of an un-ending ministry, a call to repentance, a call to give up the world and to follow Christ. Jesus is still looking for "fishermen" today. Have you answered His call?

Lord, help us to hear when You call and be willing to be obedient to whatever it is that You want us to do. Amen.

*Fishing boats along the coast of Jamaica*

# 87

## Actions and Words

But they did not obey or incline their ear, but made their neck stiff, that they might not hear nor receive instruction.

—Jeremiah 17:23 (NKJV)

Have you ever felt like God was dealing with you about something, and you said, "No! Not now!" Why did you stop God? Was it something too painful to think about or maybe a habit you were not ready to give up? Are you a Christ follower today? Do you want to grow to be who God wants you to be, or do you want to control your own life?

If we talk one way and act differently, then that is like the Pharisees of the Bible. They were religious and said all the right things, but their lives and actions were very different. They did not practice what they preached, but they were seen as righteous. In Matthew 12:33–37, Jesus says to the Pharisees:

Make a tree good and its fruit will be good, or make a tree bad and its fruit will be bad, for a tree is recognized by its fruit. You brood of vipers, how can you who are evil say anything good? For the mouth speaks what the heart is full of. A good man brings good things out of the good stored up in him, and an evil man brings evil things out of the evil stored up in him. But I tell you that everyone will have to give account on the day of judgement for every empty word they have spoken. For by your words you will be acquitted, and by your words you will be condemned. (NIV)

Second Corinthians 5:17 (NIV) says, "Therefore, if anyone is in Christ, the new creation has come: the old has gone, the new is here!"

What kind of words do you speak? Are they words that are positive and encourage or are they words that are negative and hurt those who hear them? We should be kind and considerate in all of our actions and words. Is it time for repentance? Is it time to give up control of your own life? Is it time to "let go and let God?"

I know I have just asked a lot of questions, but I have also asked myself these questions because I want to be the woman who God wants me to be. It is the difficult questions that help us to make good decisions and choices and grow in our faith. I am so thankful that, when we ask, God will forgive us and make us new. That shows how much He loves us!

Father, thank You for forgiveness, for loving us so much, and for giving us a new beginning. Amen.

# 88

## Trouble and Grace

But I want you to know, brethren, that the things
which happened to me have actually turned out for
the furtherance of the gospel.
—Philippians 1:12 (NKJV)

Most of us find ourselves going through stressful, difficult, or troubling situations from time to time. The question usually is, "What do I do? How do I handle this?" We want to do the right thing, but how do we know what that is?

Are we engaged in a spiritual battle without all of our armor? (Please read Ephesians 6:10–20 NKJV.) Is Satan trying to blind us to the truth of the situation because of our humanness, emotions, and pride? Maybe we are taking things too personally. Maybe, just maybe, God intended me to use it for my personal spiritual growth.

We need to be in prayer, asking God to lead, guide, and direct us in this situation. He may tell us to wait for His timing. That is sometimes, well, usually, difficult. I am a peacemaker, so usually when there are problems I want to immediately go to the source, discuss the issues, do what is necessary to solve the problem, and then move on. However, not everyone wants to do that because some people move at a slower pace.

Is God trying to teach me something, or is He giving me an opportunity to put into practice something He has already taught me? When trouble comes, we either use it for a stumbling block or a stepping stone.

In Philippians 1:12 (NKJV), Paul was talking about how his imprisonment had given him new opportunities to witness for Christ. When trouble comes, it can destroy our dreams or cripple our bodies. Do we react with self-pity, or do we see it as an opportunity to demonstrate the sufficiency of God's grace? Second Corinthians 12:9 states, "But he said to me, 'My grace is sufficient for you'" (NIV).

Trouble and the grace to bear it come in the same package.

Father, in our times of trouble, please give us grace and help us to see Your purpose. Amen.

# 89

## Mornings

If I take the wings of the morning, and dwell in the uttermost parts of the sea, Even there Your hand shall lead me, and Your right hand shall hold me.
—Psalm 139:9–10 (NKJV)

I was on vacation in beautiful Panama City Beach, Florida, and something very interesting happened for several mornings. I woke up early—*very early* for me because I am *not* a morning person. I was staying in a resort on the fifteenth floor, and the view was breathtaking! I could hear the surf rushing to the shore and see the birds flying close to the water in hopes of getting a meal. I could feel the warmth of the sun as I looked out at the Gulf of Mexico from my balcony. I am in awe of our heavenly Father and the beauty He gives us to enjoy.

As I looked out at the water, I thought of the power of our God. The beauty of the massive body of water is absolutely hypnotic! A pelican flew by close enough I could almost touch it, then it soared down to the water. What a beautiful bird, and it's wingspan was huge! Psalm 91 talks about the safety of abiding in the presence of God. Psalm 91:4 (TPT) says, "His massive arms are wrapped around you, protecting you. You can run under his covering of majesty and hide. His arms of faithfulness are a shield keeping you from harm."

When Jesus was on the earth, He would get up early every morning to spend time with His Father. Mark 1:35 (NKJV) tells us, "Now in the morning, having risen a long while before daylight, He went out and departed to a solitary place; and there He prayed." Jesus is our example, so if He prayed every morning to start His day, we should probably do that too. He needed His Father's guidance for the day. I find that when I start my day with God, it goes much better than when I don't.

In John 8:2 (NKJV), the Bible says, "Now early in the morning He came again into the temple, and all the people came to Him; and He sat down and taught them." *Wow*—
what a great way to start your day, being taught by Jesus! We can still have that today; all we have to do is read our Bible, pray, and spend time with our Lord first thing in the morning.

I am enjoying my mornings with God now. Are you?

Father, thank You for all the beauty You give us to enjoy and for wanting to spend time with us! Amen.

# 90

## Safety

> He who dwells in the secret place of the Most High shall abide under the shadow of the Almighty.
> —Psalm 91:1 (NKJV)

Look at only the numbers of this scripture in this psalm: 9–1–1.

Who better to call on in trying or difficult times for protection and safety than our heavenly Father! Please take time to read all of Psalm 91 (TPT)—it will bless you. It has comforting promises, and be assured God cannot and will not break His promises. God Himself speaks in this psalm. However, there are things we, too, must do to receive His promises. We must "*dwell* in the secret place of the Most High" and "a*bide* under the shadow of the Almighty" (Psalm 91:1 NKJV).

This psalm talks about how we are confident in the Lord: "He is my refuge and my fortress; My God in Him will I trust" (Psalm 91:2 NKJV). In Psalm 91:3–8 (NKJV), the psalmist talks about assurance, that if we do trust in the Lord there is no need for us to fear evil. Then in Psalm 91:9–13 (NKJV), he declares promises of God's protection, and in Psalm 91:14–16 (NKJV), he gives us a description of that protection. I don't know about you, but that certainly seems to me to be the very best place you could ever be—"under the shadow of the Almighty" (Psalm 91:1 NKJV)!

God's help, protection, and safety are always available to us *if* we love Him, obey Him, and trust Him.

Will you "Dwell in the secret place of the Most High and abide under the shadow of the Almighty" (Psalm 91:1 NKJV)?

Father God, help us to always dwell with You and abide under Your shadow. Thank You for loving us and protecting us from evil. Amen.

# Citizenship

> For our citizenship is in Heaven from which we also eagerly wait for the Savior, the Lord Jesus Christ, who will transform our lowly body, that it may be conformed to His glorious body, according to the working by which He is able even to subdue all things to Himself.
>
> —Philippians 3:20–21 (NKJV)

Paul is saying the very most important thing of all is to know Christ. (Please read Philippians 3:7–21 NKJV.) He recognizes and teaches us that true righteousness is a matter of faith, not works. He sees the value in participating in persecutions or struggles that come to those who follow Christ. Paul says to us in Philippians 3:12, "Not that I have already attained, or am already perfected; but I press on, that I may lay hold of that for which Christ Jesus has also laid hold of me" (NKJV). He could not remove the past from his memory, but he refused to let his past hinder his progress toward his goal. We as Christ followers need to remember that though we are *in* this world, we are not *of* this world; our ultimate citizenship is in heaven.

In Philippians 3:19 (NKJV), Paul presents a direct contrast to the earthly focus of the enemies of the cross. The eager desire of Christians is not earthly things but a heavenly person, the Savior, the Lord Jesus Christ.

We need to be ambassadors for Christ first and Americans second. Being an American is more of a blessing than we probably could ever imagine. However, God put each of us where we are for a reason. That is sometimes difficult to understand as we look at the world and see the poor, needy, and hurting people across the globe. We are blessed so we can bless others and share the love of Christ and what He has done for us.

Are you a Christ follower first?

Father, we cannot thank You enough for putting us where you did, to enjoy so many freedoms including freedom to worship You! Help us to love our country and each other, put You first, and look forward to our citizenship in heaven with You for eternity. Amen.

# 92

# What Is your Foundation.

Therefore whoever hears these sayings of Mine, and does them, I will liken him to a wise man who built his house on the rock.

—Matthew 7:24 (NKJV)

We all remember the story of the *Three Little Pigs* we heard growing up, then probably told our own children and maybe even our grandchildren. There is a very good lesson there that parallels the story Jesus is telling in Matthew 7:24–27 (NKJV). First, the pigs built a house with straw, then with sticks, and the *big bad wolf* destroyed them. Then they got smart and built a house with bricks where they were now safe from that big bad wolf.

In Matthew 7:26–27 (NKJV), Jesus said, "But everyone who hears these sayings of Mine, and does not do them, will be like a foolish man who built his house on the sand: and the rain descended, the floods came, and the winds blew and beat on that house; and it fell. *And great was its fall.*" What does He mean when He says, "everyone who hears these sayings of Mine"? I am so glad you asked! Jesus was a teacher and a very good speaker, and He spoke with authority. He leaves the hearers with a choice of how to live their lives. There is no better foundation than to build your life on "the Rock"—Jesus Christ. We do this first by believing He *is* the Messiah, accepting Him as our Lord and Savior, then asking for forgiveness of our sins.

Next, we are to live a life that glorifies and honors Christ and loves our fellow man. We need to read and study the Bible and share the Good News! In doing that, we are building our house upon the rock, Jesus Christ. When the storms of life come and beat on us, we will stand strong because our foundation is Christ.

When we build our lives on the foundation of Christ, our rock, the big bad wolf (Satan) cannot destroy us, try as he might.

What is your foundation?

Lord, please help us to make You our foundation so that we can stand strong when the storms of life come our way. Amen.

# 93

## Anxiety

> But he said to me, "My grace is sufficient for you, for my power is made perfect in weakness." Therefore I will boast all the more gladly about my weaknesses, so that Christ's power may rest on me.
>
> —2 Corinthians 12:9 (NIV)

Do you have situations that cause you anxiety? Most of us do from time to time. One way to describe anxiety is distress caused by fear or danger.

Some have anxiety after something has happened, such as a flat tire, missing an airline flight, or a car accident. It is normal to feel distress and even anger and other emotions in these situations. That is when we need to turn to our loving Savior for help. Philippians 4:13 (NKJV) says, "I can do all things through Christ who strengthens me." There is not one situation that Jesus can't help us with if we ask.

Satan will use whatever he can to make us fearful, steal our joy, and make our faiths falter, but we don't have to let him do that to us! In the previous scripture, Jesus says, "My power is made perfect in weakness"(2 Corinthians 12:9 NIV). When we are at our weakest is when Jesus is at His strongest! Trust Him to get us through, and that brings glory to Him and peace to us.

Lord, thank You for always being there when we need You and helping us through the tough times. Help us depend on You in our times of need. Amen.

# 94

## Through the Storm

For here is what the Lord has spoken to me: Because you have delighted in me as my great lover, I will greatly protect you. I will set you in a high place, safe and secure before my face. I will answer your cry for help every time you pray, and you will find and feel my presence even in your time of pressure and trouble. I will be your glorious hero and give you a feast.

—Psalm 91:14–15 (TPT)

I have a friend who travels with me, and we go on several adventures each year. We usually have a plan when we leave but also ask God for His plan for us. We look back and are amazed at how often God gives us favor. We start our days with Him and look for Him as we enjoy the beauty around us in His creation.

One of our trips was very different with unusual traffic delays, cooler than normal temperatures, and bad weather. We stayed positive and continued to enjoy the journey until the last hour and a half of our trip home. It began to snow, the wind was blowing harder and harder, and the flakes of snow were getting larger and larger, covering everything quickly. It was a blizzard! We were in the middle of nowhere, so we couldn't stop; there was nothing out there but darkness and snow. The road had disappeared except for two faint tire tracks on the snow-covered road. In my mind, I was crying out to God, *Father, I can't do this! I am scared!* Then the scripture in Philippians 4:13 (NIV) came to my mind: "I can do all things through Christ who gives me strength." So I kept saying that over and over in my mind. Then as the tracks became difficult to see, I asked God, "Please just give me tracks, Father! Please, please just give me tracks; then I can do this!"

In the distance, I could see two yellow flashing lights. Someone was ahead of me with their hazard lights on, so the tracks remained visible. Then I saw there was a vehicle behind me. *Thank You, Lord, that I am not alone out here in this horrible storm.* That was the longest thirty-six miles I have ever driven! But with God's help, we arrived home safely. I am convinced it was because my friend was praying, and so was I, and God heard us and answered us.

As I have reflected on this since then, Psalm 91:14–15 was made real! I now read this psalm and put my name in it. It is mine, and I claim it and receive it! God's Word is alive! It doesn't matter what storms you are going through in life—God is there. If you call on Him, He *will* answer.

What storms are you going through? Will you call on God for His help?

Father, I praise You and thank You for getting us through the storms of life, no matter what kind of storms they are. Amen.

# 95

## Listen

Blessed is the man who listens to me, watching daily at my doors, waiting at my doorway.

—Proverbs 8:34 (NIV)

In the Bible, there are many recorded stories of God interacting with people. One of my favorite stories is the story of Moses and the burning bush. Please read Exodus 3:1–12 (NIV).

In John 14:9, Jesus says to Phillip, "Jesus answered, 'Don't you know me Phillip, even after I have been among you such a long time? Anyone who has seen me has seen the Father. How can you say, Show us the Father?'" (NIV). The Bible also says in Hebrews 13:8 (NIV), "Jesus Christ is the same yesterday, and today, and forever."

I believe we can still hear from God and have encounters with Him today. He is still the same as He was then. It is important to spend time with God every day. How can we hear from Him if we don't spend time with Him? We need to shut out the noise of the world, be still, and listen.

My pastor suggests at least once a week we should find twenty minutes when we can just *listen*. When thoughts start coming, find a few words to use to make them leave, then—just listen.

God wants to commune with us. He wants an intimate relationship with us. After all, He made us. He knew us *before* He formed us in our mother's womb. Jeremiah 1:5 (NIV) says, "Before I formed you in the womb I knew you." That is what he told Jeremiah, and I believe it to be true for each of us.

Psalm 46:10 (NIV) says, "Be still and know that I am God." *Be still* is what I say when I am listening for God and the thoughts and cares of this world start to clutter my mind. I truly believe that if you listen, you *will* hear from God.

I was listening this morning, and God said to me, "Write." Not in an audible voice, but in that still, small voice in my mind that I have learned to listen to. I responded, "Okay, Father. What do You want me to write?" He gave me what I just shared with you.

Will you listen to what your heavenly Father says to you this week?

Father, please help us to make time in our busy lives to commune with You and listen to what You want to say to us. Amen.

# 96

## Air

Have you ever really thought about or pondered the word *air?* Even though it is a small word, it is full of meaning. As I researched the word (which I suggest you do as well), I found several words I liked that described it: breath, heavens, and sky.

I so love the story of creation. On day two, God created heaven and divided the waters, and while He was creating those six days, He called it *"good."*

One of my very happiest places to be is by the water, on a beach. I so enjoy looking out at the massiveness and beauty of the scene and enjoying the peacefulness it seems to bring me. Yes! It is definitely good.

One time I heard a pastor explain there are actually three heavens:

1.  The blue sky and what you see in the daytime
2.  The night sky with all the stars and planets
3.  The one beyond the two that you can see, which is the throne room of God

Paul speaks of this in 2 Corinthians 12:2 (TPT): "Someone I'm acquainted with, who is in union with Christ, was swept away fourteen years ago in an ecstatic experience. He was taken into the third heaven, but I'm not sure if he was in his body or out of his body—only God knows."

I was talking to my youngest granddaughter and telling her a little about space, the International Space Station, and astronauts. I told her the air is different in space, that the astronauts have to wear special space suits while they are in space, and that they float in the air while they are in the International Space Station. So, of course, now she wants to float! Air is vital to life; we can't live without it.

In Genesis 2:7, the scripture says, "And the Lord God formed man of the dust of the ground and breathed into his nostrils the breath of life; and man became a living being" (NKJV). I think sometimes I take some things for granted in my life. God gave us a wonderful gift when He created the earth and everything on it. Then He created us and gave us the breath of life through Adam.

Today, let us remember to be thankful for the air we breathe.

Thank You, Father, for air. Help us to be grateful for the things in life we sometimes take for granted. Amen.

# 97

## Pain

In this world you will have trouble. But take heart!
I have overcome the world.

—John 16:33 (NIV)

At the beginning of the year 2020, someone said that this would be the year of clear vision. *Wow!* I thought. *I wonder what that is going to look like.* Well, 2020 brought COVID-19, quarantine, and things I have never experienced in my seventy plus years.

Pain! Everywhere—pain. This invisible enemy causes physical pain! When lives are taken, it is a different pain. Then the fear of uncertainty comes, which causes more stress, and then that brings another kind of pain. What does it all mean? The whole world was turned upside down. Pain was everywhere!

I can't help but think that maybe God is trying to bring His children back to where they belong—to Him. Is that what is happening? A big part of the world does not acknowledge God. Is He trying to reach a deaf world? He loves His children and wants to have a personal relationship with each one.

In the Passion Translation, John 16:33 says:

And everything I've taught you is so that the peace which is in me will be in you and will give you great confidence as you rest in me. For in this unbelieving world you will experience trouble and sorrows, but you must be courageous, for I have conquered the world!

This scripture is full of instruction, truth, and hope. John 16:29–33 talks about being taught by Jesus, believing in Him, and having peace in tribulation. In the world there is tribulation; in Jesus there is peace—even in the midst of tribulation.

Will you trust Jesus and His Word?

Father, we thank You for Your Word, which brings hope and peace in these troubling times. Help us to do our part to show Jesus to a hurting world. Amen.

# 98

# The Sand Dollar

But He was wounded for our transgressions, He was bruised for our iniquities.

—Isaiah 53:5 (NKJV)

The legend of the sand dollar is fascinating to me. It tells that the five slits on the shell represent the wounds Christ suffered on the cross. That made me think of the above scripture in Isaiah. Also, on the front of the shell is the Easter lily with a star in the middle, which represents the Star of Bethlehem. On the back is the outline of the poinsettia, the Christmas flower, and on the inside are five doves. When the shell is carefully broken open, these five doves form a star and are a symbol of spreading good will and peace *after* being *broken* open.

Christ's body was broken, and His blood was shed for us. We are to remember this through the institution of the Lord's Supper found in 1 Corinthians 11:23–26, which says:

> For I received from the Lord that which I also delivered to you; that the Lord Jesus on the same night in which He was betrayed took bread; and when He had given thanks, He broke it and said, "Take, eat, this is My body which is broken for you; do this in remembrance of Me." In the same manner

He also took the cup after supper, saying, "This cup is the new covenant in My blood. This do, as often as you drink it, in remembrance of me. For as often as you eat this bread and drink this cup, you proclaim the Lord's death till He comes." (NKJV)

At some point in time, the beautiful white sand dollar shells have been alive, and it is when they die we can see them and the story they tell. We humans should tell our story while we are alive. By that I mean share with others what Jesus has done and is doing in our lives so others may be encouraged and maybe even some brought to Christ.

All nature seems to tell of God's majesty. The sand dollar shell tells the story of Christ, and we should be telling it, too, and praising God for His excellent greatness! I thank God for nature, its beauty, and how it points us to Him—our awesome God!

Father God, thank You for nature and the beauty You have created with its many stories that point back to You. Amen.

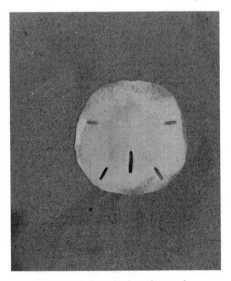

*Sand dollar shell in the sand*

# 99

## Always Learning

Do not conform to the pattern of this world, but be transformed by the renewing of your mind. Then you will be able to test and approve what God's will is—his good, pleasing and perfect will.
—Romans 12:2 (NIV)

The COVID-19 pandemic we experienced touched the lives of everyone in one way or another. It turned the whole world as we knew it upside down. It has been said there is always something good that comes out of something bad, and I am an optimist. I like to believe that is true—so what good can come from a pandemic that has been so devastating for so many?

Well, for one thing, people helped each other. It seems like the world is full of hate and anger, but in a crisis, people step up and help people in need. Another is that this pandemic made people creative in ways that would not have been imagined otherwise. Look at Zoom! It is helping us to stay connected.

People have been so fearful. I believe we need to follow the advice of the professionals to keep ourselves and others safe but not live in fear. The Bible says in
2 Timothy 1:7, "For God has not given us a spirit of fear, but of power and of love and of a sound mind" (NKJV). For me, staying

home more allowed me to spend even more time with God, be in the Word more, and pray more. In doing this, it kept me from being fearful and strengthened my faith. In Romans 12:2, it talks about the renewing of your mind, and I believe that means reading and studying God's Word. Praying will help us to do that. Then in the second half of the verse, it gives you the results of what happens when you do what the scripture says: "Then you will be able to test and approve what God's will is—his good, pleasing, and perfect will"(Romans 12:2 NIV).

I want God's perfect will for my life while respecting and following the recommendations set for us by the CDC and other professionals, as long as those recommendations do not go against God. We can and should be aways learning, renewing our minds with God's Word to help us walk by faith in our daily lives and be in God's perfect will.

What will you learn today?

Father, thank You for another day to live, learn, and draw closer to You and those we love. Amen.

# Author Introduction

I was blessed to go to Israel a few years after my husband went to be with Jesus. It had been a long time dream of mine to visit the Holy Land and my Awesome God had it planned at the perfect time. It was beneficial to my healing and returning to the woman that God wanted me to be after my precious husband died. Going to Israel and seeing where Jesus walked, lived, and taught was an experience that changed my life and brought much needed healing. Mourning the loss of your spouse is not something you *get over* but rather something that you work through daily and learn to live with.

It was during that time that I began to write. I would get up in the morning, have my coffee with God, read His Word, then be inspired to write. I thank Him and praise Him for the opportunity to share with others what He has put on my heart. My prayer is that the meditations that I write will *encourage, inspire, and challenge* those who read them.